Research Report 30
December 2002

The arts in the early years:
a national study of policy and practice

Alison Clark, Ellen Heptinstall,
Antonia Simon and Peter Moss

Contents

Title	Page
Acknowledgements	5
Conventions	6
Glossary	7
Executive summary	9
1 Introduction	**13**
1.1 Aims and objectives of the study	13
1.2 Background	13
1.3 Context	13
1.4 Components of the study	15
2 The role of the arts in work with young children	**20**
2.1 Aims for the arts and young children	20
2.2 What are the benefits for parents and communities?	24
2.3 What are the benefits for early years professionals?	26
2.4 What are the benefits for artists and arts organisations?	27
2.5 Discussion and conclusion	28
3 Policies, staffing and structure	**31**
3.1 Policy and staffing	31
3.2 Training	34
3.3 Networks	38
3.4 Funding	39
3.5 Collaboration	41
3.6 Future plans	44
3.7 Discussion and conclusion	44
4 Practice in the arts in the early years	**47**
4.1 Key projects	47
4.2 Artforms explored	48
4.3 Participants	52
4.4 Providers of the activities	53
4.5 Settings for the activities	55
4.6 Knowledge about the wider arts context	58
4.7 Discussion and conclusion	59
5 Case studies	**61**
5.1 Background and inspiration	61
5.2 Organisation	62
5.3 Funding and collaboration	63
5.4 Children's role	63
5.5 Parental involvement	64

	5.6 Follow up	64
	5.7 Evaluation	64
6	**National priorities**	**65**
	6.1 Factors encouraging the arts and early years	65
	6.2 Factors hindering the arts in the early years	67
	6.3 National priorities	69
	6.4 The role of the Arts Council	74
7	**Discussion and future directions**	**77**
	7.1 The role of the arts in the early years	77
	7.2 Curriculum balance	78
	7.3 Policies, structures and staffing	79
	7.4 Funding	80
	7.5 Training	80
	7.6 Artforms	81
	7.7 Conclusion	81
8	**References**	**83**

Appendix One - The arts in the early years questionnaire　　85

Appendix Two - Focus group participants　　99

Appendix Three - The case studies　　102

　　Case study one　　102
　　Case study two　　105
　　Case study three　　108
　　Case study four　　111
　　Case study five　　113
　　Case study six　　116
　　Case study seven　　119
　　Case study eight　　121
　　Case study nine　　124
　　Case study ten　　126

List of Tables

Table   **Page**

Table 1.1: Groups included in the survey sample 16

Table 1.2: The number of questionnaires sent out to each type of organisation and the response rate of the return 17

Table 1.3: The number of questionnaires sent to groups in each area covered by the Arts Council regional offices and the response rate 17

Table 3.1: Percentage of respondents who said their organisation has a policy on arts in the early years 32

Table 3.2: Artforms included in policies for the arts in the early years 32

Table 3.3: Areas of work covered by arts in the early years policies 32

Table 3.4: Percentage of respondents whose organisation has a designated person with responsibility for developing arts in the early years 33

Table 3.5: Percentage of each group of respondents who have a designated person with responsibility for developing arts in the early years 33

Table 3.6: Percentage of groups providing training in the arts and early years during the past 12 months 34

Table 3.7: Percentage of respondents from each group who have provided training 35

Table 3.8: Percentage of organisations which have a policy and have provided training .. 36

Table 3.9: Percentage of respondents receiving funding for the arts and the early years . 39

Table 3.10: Percentage of most frequently identified funding sources 39

Table 3.11: Percentage of funding sources accessed by arts and education sector organisations 40

Table 3.12: Case study collaboration 43

Table 3.13: Percentage of respondents who said their organisation had specific plans for developing the arts in the early years 44

Table 4.1: Examples of the types of key projects 48

Table 4.2: Artforms included in the key projects by type of organisation 51

Table 4.3: Participants in arts activities 52

Table 4.4: Participants in arts activities, by type of organisation or programme 52

Table 4.5: Individuals/organisations used as providers by type of organisation or programme 54

Table 4.6: Venues used by respondents for arts provision 55

Table 4.7: The use of schools, curriculum development centres and libraries
as venues for arts provision by type of organisation 56

Table 4.8: The use of galleries, theatres and museums as venues for arts
provision, by type of organisation 57

Table 4.9: Knowledge of arts organisations working with young children in respondents'
local areas 58

Table 4.10: Knowledge of arts organisations working with young children in
respondents' local areas, by type of group..58

Table 5.1: Ten case studies listed by region 62

Table 6.1: Six areas identified as a national priority for developing the arts in
the early years, in descending order 70

Acknowledgements

The Steering Group for this project was:

- Shirley Campbell (Chair), Arts Council of England, Northern Regional Office
- Karen Dust, Arts Council of England National Office
- Sally Giddings, Arts Council of England, South West Regional Office
- Barry Hepton, Arts Council of England, North West Regional Office
- Hassina Khan, Arts Council of England National Office

with additional support from Helen McNamara, Department for Education and Skills.

We would like to thank the children, artists and early years practitioners who took part in the case studies, with special thanks to those who organised our project visits:

- Robin Duckett, Sightlines Initiative, Newcastle
- Catherine Richardson, Wolsey Gallery, Christchurch Mansion, Ipswich
- Lisa Mead, Education Officer, The Croydon Clocktower
- Claire Ackroyd, Bradford Education
- Pat Hickman and Chris Morgan, Music and Dance Education, Marazion, Cornwall
- Nikki-Kate Heyes, soundLINCS
- Ann Clay, Hillfields Early Years Centre, Coventry
- Rosie Marcus, Artists in Schools, Bolton
- Marion East, Early Years Development and Childcare Partnership, Isle of Wight
- Ronessa Knock, Arts Education Service, Essex County Council

Conventions

Number in each table refers to the number of people answering/stating a particular category.

Base refers to the total number of respondents who answered a particular question. In tables that show questions where more than one option could have been chosen by respondents, the base can be lower than the numbers answering each category.

Percentages quoted in the report may add to 99% or 100% because of rounding.

Case study examples appear in shaded boxes.

Glossary

Arts Council of England national and regional offices	On 1 April 2002, the Arts Council of England and the 10 Regional Arts Boards joined together to form a single development organisation for the arts, with a national office and nine regional offices.
Arts Education Agency	Agency which acts as a broker between arts organisations and schools
'atelierista'	Trained artist working as an integral part of early learning in the pre-schools of Reggio Emilia
Curriculum Development Centre	Centre for continuing professional development of education professionals
Early Excellence Centre	Early childhood centre developing a range of good practice in integrated early education and childcare, with the support and involvement of parents and carers and other family services
Early Years Development and Childcare Partnership	Local partnerships of service providers and stakeholders, covering early education and out-of-school and holiday provision for children from 0-14
Education Action Zone	A Government scheme targeting extra resources on groups of schools to raise educational standards in areas of disadvantage
Early Learning Goals	Expected attainment for most children by the end of the Foundation Stage, in each of the six areas of learning: personal, social and emotional development; communication, language and literacy; mathematical development; knowledge and understanding of the world; physical development; and creative development.
Foundation Stage Curriculum	Six areas of learning to cover the period from age three to the end of the reception year
Maintained setting	Early years provision in receipt of direct funding from the Local Education Authority (LEA)
Neighbourhood Nursery	Government initiative to provide full daycare for children from birth to school age in disadvantaged communities

The arts in the early years

Non-maintained setting	Early years provision not directly attached to an LEA and not in receipt of LEA funding
OFSTED	Government body responsible for the inspection of schools and all registered childcare and early years education
Reggio Emilia	A town in Northern Italy with an international reputation for early childhood education, described as 'the Reggio approach'. Practice in these municipal infant-toddler centres and pre-schools is based on the idea that creativity is a central component of thinking and of responding to the world.
Residency	Artist or arts organisation working in a particular place over a period of time
Standards Fund	A collection of specific government grants designed to enable schools and LEAs to achieve improvements in education standards; these are set out in agreed targets
Sure Start	A Government scheme set up to improve the health and well-being of children under four years old, and their families, living in areas of disadvantage. Local Sure Start programmes provide family support, childcare and early learning opportunities. Good practice learned from local programmes will be spread to others providing services for young children

The arts in the early years

Executive summary

In 2002, the Arts Council of England commissioned the Thomas Coram Research Unit, at the University of London Institute of Education, to conduct a national study of the arts in the early years (children from birth to six years old). The overall aim was to collect the views of key providers in the arts and early years sectors to help provide a firm foundation for development work in this area. The research also aimed to identify and describe examples of current practice in the arts in the early years.

The research has been carried out at a time of structural and curriculum change in the early years sector. For example, Early Years Development and Childcare Partnerships (EYDCPs) have been created at local authority level and the new Government, area-based Sure Start programmes focus on children under four and their families. The Foundation Stage Curriculum for children from three to six years includes creative development as one of six key curriculum areas and has clear implications for the teaching of the arts.

There are also several national initiatives to raise the profile of the arts within education, including Artsmark, the Arts Education Interface, Space for Sport and Arts and Creative Partnerships. (For more information see the Arts Council of England website: www.artscouncil.org.uk)

There were three strands to the research.

1. **A national survey** of arts education and early years representatives to identify, and collect the views of, key providers of arts and early years activity and to identify examples of current practice. The sample included arts education agencies, regional arts offices, Education Action Zones, Sure Start Trailblazer programmes and regional managers, EYDCPs, EECs, LEA early years advisers and inspectors, and representatives from national early years organisations and children's charities. The analysis is based on 204 returns, giving a response rate of 37%.

2. **Six focus groups** of representatives from the arts and early years sectors to discuss current practice and future priorities. There were five regional groups and one national group which was attended by representatives of national early years and arts organisations and relevant Government departments: the Department for Education and Skills (DfES), the Sure Start Unit and the Department for Culture, Media and Sport (DCMS).

3. **Ten case studies** of current practice in the arts in the early years.

The role of the arts

- The views expressed in this research reveal a strong belief in the value of the arts in the early years. Ninety-two per cent of respondents regarded increasing self-esteem and encouraging creative thinking as 'very important' aims.

- More than three-quarters of respondents (78%) saw learning through the arts as a 'very important' aim. The arts had an intrinsic value but were also seen as being a useful gateway to learning in other subjects.

- Respondents reported benefits to parents when their children were involved in the arts, including opportunities to become involved in their children's learning and the chance for self-expression.

- Benefits to early years professionals and artists included the inspiration gained from working with other professionals and new challenges for their own practice and assumptions.

Policy, structure and staffing

- Eighty per cent of respondents had specific plans for developing the arts in the early years. However, only a minority had structures in place to facilitate this: just a quarter of respondents had policies on arts in the early years and only 29% had designated staff with responsibility for developing arts in the early years work.
- Training for both arts and early years practitioners was seen as crucial to the development of arts practice with young children. Seventy-one per cent of respondents had provided training in this area during the last 12 months. Respondents indicated that there were fewer relevant training opportunities for artists than for early years practitioners.

- Specialist networks strengthened collaboration between the arts and early years sectors, although only 19% of respondents belonged to such a network. More respondents belonged to a general arts education network (43%).

- Half of the respondents had received specific funding for the arts and early years during the past 12 months. The four most frequently quoted funding sources were from the education sector. Some respondents (14%) had received funding through the Regional Arts Lottery Programme (RALP).

- Despite the range of funding sources available, respondents indicated that funding for arts in the early years was often fragmented and short term, with funding for each new project often coming from several sources.

Current practice

- The study reveals an exciting range of current practice involving the arts and the early years. Almost three-quarters of respondents (71%) had included music in work with young children; 68% had included visual arts and crafts. Literature and media/multi-media were mentioned less frequently.

The arts in the early years

- There was a stronger emphasis on involving the three to six years age group than on involving the under threes. Relatively few respondents were using museums, galleries and theatres as settings for arts activities, although there were examples of this in the case studies.

Case studies

Respondents provided details of 164 key arts in the early years projects. Three-quarters of these involved more than one artform.

Ten case studies were selected from the key projects, including one example from each of the areas covered by the nine Arts Council of England regional offices. A tenth example was chosen to illustrate a network established between artists, early years professionals and an arts organisation. The case studies covered the following initiatives:

- A long-term project involving artists, early years staff, parents and young children based on practice in the pre-schools of Reggio Emilia in Italy.
- An interactive gallery project with outreach elements.
- A participatory project in a public space.
- A visual artist and a dance group working with young children and parents.
- A dance and music partnership involving an arts organisation, an EYDCP and Sure Start.
- An early years music programme across one county.
- An artist residency in an Early Excellence Centre, linked to a gallery.
- Residencies based on collaboration between the Early Years Advisory Service, an EYDCP and an Artists-in-Schools agency.
- A collaboration with an arts organisation and early years settings combining literature and the visual arts.
- A network model of training and residencies for artists and early years staff.

National priorities

Respondents to the survey, and participants in the focus groups, identified the following factors which were seen to have encouraged work in the arts and early years:
- New funding opportunities
- Inspirational theory and practice in the UK and abroad
- Exchange and debate
- Structural change, including the creation of EYDCPs
- Curriculum change, including the creation of the Foundation Stage

Respondents and participants identified the following negative factors:
- Status of the arts in the early years
- Funding problems
- Training issues across the diverse early years sector
- Structural difficulties making it difficult to reach the whole early years sector
- 'Measurement culture'

The arts in the early years

- Access problems

There was particular concern that short-term project funding, rather than core funding, could hinder long-term development.

The study highlighted some key areas for development:
- Collaboration between the early years and arts sectors
- Raising the status of the early years and arts sectors
- Funding
- Training and dissemination
- Inclusion and access

The Government, the Arts Council and EYDCPs were each seen to have an important role in the future development of the arts in the early years. Key areas include research, funding, training and dissemination.

Areas for development

- Research into the benefits of the arts
- Research into how much arts work with young children is taking place in Sure Start programmes and EAZs
- Pilot schemes using the Reggio Emilia approach
- Exploration of the potential for core funding for the arts in the early years
- Protection of the place of the arts within initial teacher training and reinforcement of the role of the arts in the Foundation Stage
- Models of training for artists and early years professionals
- Promotion of the use of the new Arts Council grants, available from April 2003, for the arts in the early years
- Liaison between EYDCPs and the Arts Council to disseminate good practice between regions and nationally
- Arts specialists in each EYDCP to promote the arts in the early years

– **The arts in the early years**

1 Introduction

This report outlines a national study of arts activities in the early years (children from birth to six years old). The Arts Council of England commissioned Thomas Coram Research Unit, which is part of the Institute of Education at the University of London, to carry out this study. The purpose was to collect information about current initiatives and investigate future possibilities for development, including funding and research.

1.1 Aims and objectives of the study

The aim of the research was to identify, and collect the views of, key providers of arts and early years activity in order to provide a firm foundation for the development of work in this area.

The objectives of the research were to:

- Identify key providers and agencies from both the arts and early years sectors at a national and regional level
- Produce a detailed analysis of existing and planned priorities and programmes across both the arts and early years sectors
- Identify potential partners and areas for further research and development

1.2 Background

This current study follows previous research commissioned by The Arts Council and Northern Arts to examine creativity and the development of young children between three and six years of age. Two pieces of work were undertaken: a literature review of research and current thinking in this field (Sharp, 2001) and a mapping of recent work involving young children and the arts in the Northern Arts region (Redmond, 2001).

There is a growing interest in arts work with young children and a concomitant rise in the level of information being collected. For example, the Arts Council regional office in the West Midlands has undertaken a regional study of artists in early learning (Godfrey, 2001), and Simpson (2000) conducted a national survey of arts organisations and their work with young children.

This research adds to the earlier studies the views of early years practitioners and policy makers, managers from Sure Start programmes and those in Education Action Zones (EAZs). It also includes the views of the Arts Council regional offices and arts education agencies.

1.3 Context

A study of the arts and the early years is concerned with the impact of the arts on young children's lives now and in the future, whether as consumers, makers, performers or audience. At an international level, the arts and the early years are

The arts in the early years

part of wider discussions about children's rights. The United Nations Convention on the Rights of the Child (1989) states that every child has the right to participate freely in cultural life and the arts (Article 13). There is also a growing body of evidence to support the role of the arts in stimulating young children's cognitive, motor, language and social-emotional development (Gardner, 1993; Clark, 1998; Eisner, 1998).

> The arts are natural for young children. Child development specialists note that play is the business of young children: play is the way children promote and enhance their development. The arts are a most natural vehicle for play.
>
> Task Force on Children's Learning and the Arts: Birth to age eight (Arts Education Partnership, Massachusetts,1998)

The arts can be one means through which young children develop their creativity and imagination (Duffy, 1998). The relationship between the arts and creativity has been the source of much debate (Prentice, 2000; Sharp, 2001). The focus in this study is on arts activities rather than developing creativity, although as the Robinson Report (1999) points out, the expressive arts are a central factor in exploring creativity.

Changes within the early years sector have opened up new possibilities for arts work with young children. In England, the Foundation Stage Curriculum, introduced for children aged three to six years, includes 'creative development' as one of six areas of learning (the Early Learning Goals). Curriculum guidance from the Qualifications and Curriculum Authority (QCA) on effective creative development includes reference to the arts and in particular the need to provide opportunities for children to 'work alongside artists and other creative adults'. (QCA, 2000).

Early Years Development and Childcare Partnerships (EYDCPs) have been created. Operating at local authority level, they bring together service providers and other stakeholders to plan early education and out-of-school and holiday activities for children up to the age of 14. Part-time education provision has been extended to include three and four year olds. Other initiatives include the setting up of Early Excellence Centres (EECs) and Neighbourhood Nurseries. The Government's Sure Start programme also focuses on the early years, offering new configurations of services for children under four, and their families, in areas of disadvantage.

Other Government initiatives relating to improving school effectiveness and tackling social exclusion may also have had an impact on provision for young children: for example, EAZs. Organisational change within the education sector has brought new funding opportunities for work with young children and the possibility of new partnerships to develop arts provision.

Learning through the arts in the early years has been influenced by early childhood practice abroad. The pre-schools of Reggio Emila in Italy present a particular model of learning which promotes the expressive arts as tools for developing children's thinking (Edwards, 1998). The approach includes integrating artists' studios into early years settings and giving young children the opportunity to work with artists or 'atelieristas' as an everyday feature of exploring the world. There has not been a national pilot of this approach in the UK; however, a growing number of early years practitioners have been influenced by these ideas and are adapting the Reggio approach for their own practice (Abbott and Nutbrown, 2001).

At a national level, there are currently several initiatives to raise the profile of the arts within education. Artsmark[1] is a national arts award for primary, middle, secondary and special schools in England. It aims to give recognition to schools with a proven commitment to the arts, offering an Artsmark award at three levels: Artsmark, Artsmark Silver or Artsmark Gold.

The Arts Education Interface is a three-year action research project funded by the Arts Council. It is exploring the impact of different types of arts intervention on children and young people in EAZs in Bristol and Corby.

Spaces for Sport and Arts is a £130 million initiative to build sports and arts spaces in up to 300 primary schools across England. Jointly funded by the Government and the Lottery (through Sport England, the Arts Council and the New Opportunities Fund), it aims to meet the needs of schools and local communities.

Creative Partnerships is a Government initiative, led by the Arts Council, to develop partnerships between schools and the creative industries in 16 pilot areas across England. While Creative Partnerships does not include the early years, the initiative will have an indirect impact on early years settings based in schools.

1.4 Components of the study

The study, which took place between January and July 2002, has three main components:

- A national survey of arts education and early years representatives, to explore current practice and gather views about future priorities for the arts in the early years
- Six focus groups (five regional groups and one for national organisations) bringing together representatives from the arts and early years sectors to discuss current practice and future priorities
- Ten case studies of current arts and early years practice

---

[1] see the Arts Council website for more details of this and other initiatives: www.artscouncil.org.uk

The arts in the early years

The national survey

The aim was to gather views and experiences of the arts and the early years across both sectors.

Table 1.1: Groups included in the survey sample

Groups	Notes
Arts Council Regional Offices	Education Officers. On 1st April 2002, during the period of this research, the Arts Council of England and the ten Regional Arts Boards joined together to form a single development organisation. This new structure comprises a national office and nine regional offices.
Arts Education Agencies	National and regional arts education agencies were identified through the regional offices
Early Years Development and Childcare Partnerships	Lead Officers in the Early Years Development and Childcare Partnerships
Local Education Authority advisers/inspectors for the early years	Some LEAs have a combined Advisory and Inspection service. Early years advisers in some LEAs are now working as part of the EYDCPs, in which case the survey was sent to the EYDCP
Sure Start	Sure Start regional managers and managers of the first sixty Sure Start programmes or 'Trailblazers'
Education Action Zones	The Project Directors of all EAZs established in the first two rounds of funding were included
Early Excellence Centres	Heads of each centre.
National early years organisations and national children's charities.	These national organisations were all engaged in work with young children

To keep the sample size manageable, groups working primarily at a national, regional or local authority level were targeted. However, the sample also included two types of locally-based provision: Sure Start programmes and EECs.

Table 1.2: The number of questionnaires sent out to each type of organisation and the response rate of the return

Type of organisation	Number of questionnaires sent	Number returned	Response rate (percentage)
Sure Start	68	26	38
Education Action Zone	74	17	23
Early Excellence Centre	54	23	43
Early Years Development and Childcare Partnership	148	56	38
Local Education Authority	112	39	35
Arts Education Agency	67	26	39
Arts Council Regional Office	10	8	80
National children's charities/early years organisation	22	9	41
Base	555	204	37

Questionnaires were sent to 555 organisations. Completed questionnaires were received from 204 respondents, giving a response rate of 37%.

Table 1.3: The number of questionnaires sent to groups in each area covered by the Arts Council regional offices and the response rate

Regional Offices	Number of questionnaires sent	Number returned	Response rate (percentage)
Northern Arts	46	23	50
Yorkshire Arts	63	22	35
North West Arts	74	24	32
East Midlands Arts	40	18	45
West Midlands Arts	53	17	32
East England Arts	36	13	36
London Arts	131	36	27
Southern &South East Arts	66	32	48
South West Arts	46	19	41
Base	555	204	37

The Northern Arts region (50%) and the Southern & South East Arts region (48%) returned the highest proportion of responses.

Focus groups

Respondents from both the arts and early years sectors were invited to attend focus groups to discuss issues raised in the questionnaires. There was wide interest in taking part in these discussions. One hundred and sixty-four respondents expressed an interest in participating; 70 places were available.

A national focus group brought together representatives from national early years and arts organisations and relevant Government departments. The Department for Culture, Media and Sport (DCMS), the Department for Education and Skills (DfES) and the Sure Start Unit attended.

Five regional groups were held in York, Peterborough, Manchester, Exeter and London, between them covering all regional office areas. Group participants included those who were working at a policy level, such as EYDCP lead officers and LEA advisers, and those working directly with young children. Representatives of the regional offices were present at each of the focus groups.

Discussion focused on the rationale for the arts with young children, current practice and future development. Participants were able to draw on their experiences of current policy and practice to discuss these issues. Two researchers from the study took part in the focus groups, one acting as facilitator and the second as note-taker. Five of the six group discussions were tape-recorded; full transcriptions were made.

Case studies

Respondents to the national survey were asked to identify one or two examples of current, recent or future key projects which demonstrated how young children were being involved in gaining skills in the arts, knowledge about the arts or learning through the arts. Ten case studies were selected from the resulting list to illustrate a range of current practice. The selection criteria were:

- Projects involving different partnerships between the arts and early years sectors
- Projects taking place in a range of arts and early years settings
- A range of geographical locations, including inner city, small town, rural and coastal locations
- A variety of artforms
- A range of project types to include artist residencies, training, conferences and workshops
- Projects involving children as audience as well as in 'hands-on' activities
- Projects promoting cultural diversity and inclusion

One case study was chosen from each of the nine regional office areas. A tenth case study was selected to illustrate a network established between artists, an arts organisation and the early years sector.

Researchers travelled to each of the regions to meet with the organisers of the case-study projects. A detailed interview was conducted with the organisers and supplementary material gathered, including project evaluations if they were available. The researchers were able to meet with and conduct observations of young children engaged in the arts in those projects which were ongoing. They also carried out interviews with some of the artists and early years practitioners involved in the projects.

The report

The report is divided into the following sections. The material has been drawn from the questionnaire survey, the focus groups and the case studies.

- Section 2 looks at the role of the arts in the early years. It examines different perspectives on the benefits of the arts for young children, parents and communities, early years professionals and artists
- Section 3 focuses on policies, structure and staffing in the arts in the early years. This includes an investigation of training, networks and funding
- Section 4 provides an overview of current practice and discusses artforms, providers, settings for arts activities and knowledge about the wider arts context
- Section 5 presents an overview of the ten case studies illustrating work in the arts in the early years. Detailed descriptions of the case studies are included in Appendix Three
- Section 6 builds on this by examining respondents' views about national priorities. These are discussed together with the other findings in Section 7, which includes recommendations for future research and development

The report gives an overview of current practice. The reported findings refer to all respondents but any significant differences between different groups or regions are highlighted. It has seldom been possible to find statistical differences between regions due to the small data sets. Other differences may be mentioned as worthy of future research using a larger sample.

2 The role of the arts in work with young children

This section looks at perceptions of the role of the arts in early years education.

What should be the aims for the arts in the early years? Can involvement in the arts for this age group also have a wider impact on parents and communities? Our discussion about aims leads into a consideration of the benefits of the arts in the early years for parents and communities, early years professionals and artists, as well as for the children themselves. These issues are covered as follows:

2.1 Aims for the arts and young children. How important are the arts for promoting young children's social, emotional, cognitive and physical development?

2.2 Benefits for parents and communities. What is the wider impact of involving young children in the arts?

2.3 Benefits for early years professionals? How is their own practice influenced?

2.4 Benefits for artists and arts organisations? What is the impact on their work?

2.5 Discussion and conclusion.

Survey respondents were asked: 'In your view, which of these aims are important for the arts in the early years?' They were asked to rank a list of 12 aims relating to children, parents and the whole school, early years professionals and artists, as 'very important', 'important', 'not very important' and 'not important at all'.

2.1 Aims for the arts and young children

The aims relating to young children and the percentage of respondents who considered them to be 'very important' were:

- Increasing self esteem (92%)
- Encouraging creative thinking (92%)
- Listening to young children (86%)
- Providing fun and celebrating achievement (82%)
- Developing learning through the arts (78%)
- Increasing knowledge about the world (56%)
- Developing skills in the arts (50%)
- Developing knowledge about the arts (31%)

Increasing self esteem

This aspect of children's emotional and social development was seen as one of the most important aims of arts work with young children. Many respondents mentioned the opportunities offered by the arts for children to succeed.

> … raises some children's self esteem and confidence – it can't be wrong.
>
> Early Excellence Centre staff

> There is no right or wrong, so self-esteem is high – the child is creating, not simply copying.
>
> LEA Adviser

The therapeutic value of the arts was mentioned by some respondents, particularly those working on Government initiatives in areas of disadvantage. The arts were seen to have therapeutic value for both young children and their parents.

Several respondents took the notion of self-esteem a step further and showed how this could be linked to increased self-knowledge.

> Developing confidence in themselves as 'actors in their own universe' – personal agency.
>
> Education Action Zone staff

Listening to children can also play a part in raising their self-esteem. More than four-fifths of respondents (86%) regarded listening as another 'very important' aim for work with young children in the arts.

Encouraging creative thinking

Encouraging cognitive development through creative thinking was seen as a 'very important' aim by over nine-tenths of respondents. Encouraging young children's creative thinking was described by respondents as exploring new ideas, 'no wrong answers' and as a 'gateway' to other subjects.

Exploring new ideas

Respondents described the arts as providing the context within which young children can explore new ideas and make connections with previous knowledge.

> …[the arts] provide opportunities to experiment, explore, reflect and respond – to make choices and to test them.
>
> Arts Education Officer

> Arts involvement provides a creative contact for higher order skills – independent working, collaborating, problem-solving, decision-making, communicating, creative thought.
>
> Education Action Zone staff

Gateway to other subjects

Respondents commented on how thinking skills developed through the arts can then influence children's approaches to other curriculum areas.

> The arts can be a gateway to the whole curriculum.
>
> Early Excellence Centre staff

Others referred to the arts promoting curiosity, which again can be applied across other disciplines.

> [The arts] give learning back to the children.
>
> Early years professional

Fun and celebration

Respondents recognised the importance of the fun experienced by young children engaged in the arts. Just over four-fifths of respondents (82%) saw providing fun and celebrating achievement as very important aims. The need to protect this aspect of the arts, creating spaces in which children could play and be themselves, was discussed by participants in the focus groups (see discussion below).

Learning skills in the arts, knowledge about the arts or learning through the arts?

More than three-quarters of respondents (78%) saw learning **through** the arts as a 'very important' aim for young children. This links to the views expressed about enhancing creative thinking, where the arts act as a gateway to other subjects. Less importance was attached to young children developing skills **in** the arts, with only half of the respondents ranking this as ' very important' aim. The least importance was attached to developing knowledge **about** the arts, such as learning about individual artists and the history of the arts; less than a third (31%) of respondents saw this as a 'very important' aim for arts in the early years.

Improving communication skills

Respondents were also given the opportunity to suggest other aims which, in their opinion, were important for the arts in the early years. Respondents drew attention to the importance of the arts for young children in improving communication skills.

Respondents reported the value of the arts in promoting young children's listening skills, speech development and non-verbal communication. Music was described as an important factor in speech development. Other respondents mentioned the range of arts media or tools which children could use to develop their communication skills.

> Offering to children languages with which they are able to express and communicate ideas and feelings.
>
> Arts Education Officer

The arts were seen as a way of helping all children to develop their communication skills regardless of their academic ability.

> As a means of enabling all children to find a voice, a means of expression which is non-threatening and transcends any special needs they may have.
>
> Early Excellence Centre staff

There were several examples of young children who had talked for the first time in a pre-school setting as a direct result of participation in an arts activity.

Focus group comments on the benefits of the arts for young children

Participants in the focus groups emphasised how exploring the arts can provide young children with an arena for experimenting and taking risks, without the anxiety of needing to 'get it right'. However, participants also emphasised that such freedom was dependent on artists and early years professionals reinforcing this open way of learning.

> Creativity is a process of collaboration between artists and children. I don't teach specific skills [out of context]. The children realise their own ideas and how you involve skills [what skills are needed].
>
> Artist

> It can lead to a huge improvement in self-esteem with children. But of course, the converse is also true: where practitioners are not sensitive to or understanding of creativity, it can have a bad effect, by saying, 'This isn't the way it actually ought to be. Rabbits look like this'. It is a two-edged sword.
>
> Early years professional

Focus group participants reinforced the importance of the arts for improving young children's communication skills. Several examples showed how involvement in an arts activity had been the catalyst for a breakthrough in communication. The following incident was described by an artist from a theatre company which was working with a nursery school. The company was running a participatory project on the theme of making houses.

> …We asked them to dress up as builders, little builders' hats and things like that. Over the first day we began to make friends. We began to talk and on

the second day, one little boy came up to one of the builders and said, 'Can I have some of your tinsel to put on my hat?' So she was delighted to give him some of her tinsel and he put it on his hat. And afterwards the head of the nursery came up and said, 'That was fantastic'. And we said, 'Well why?' and she said, 'He has been in this nursery for two terms and that is the first thing he has said'.

Participants in the focus groups also discussed the inclusive nature of learning through the arts. The benefits for young children with special needs and those for whom English is an additional language were raised.

Discussion in the focus groups also pointed to the value of the arts in opening up different cultures and celebrating heritage with young children (see Case Study Four).

2.2   What are the benefits for parents and communities?

Included in the list of aims were two relating to parents, the school and the wider community:

- Involving parents and the wider community (considered 'very important' by 63% of respondents)
- Promoting a positive image of the school/area (considered 'very important' by 41%)

More emphasis was placed on involving parents and their communities than promoting a positive image of the school or area. The aim relating to parents and communities was considered 'important' by those from both the early years and arts sectors. However, this aim was of particular importance for respondents from Government initiatives, which have a strong parental dimension. Twenty-two of the 26 Sure Start programmes saw this as 'very important', together with 11 of the 17 EAZs.

Focus group comments on the wider benefits for parents and communities

Participants discussed the benefits for parents and communities in terms of:

- Parental involvement in their children's learning
- Parental self-expression
- Impact on the wider community

Parental involvement

Participants discussed how the arts can provide a new way for parents to engage with their child's learning.

> It encourages parents to celebrate their children's achievements. It gives them confidence to build on children's development.
>
> Arts Education Officer
>
> It breaks down barriers, gets the whole family involved in shared activities and gives the children a voice.
>
> Arts Education Officer

Parental involvement was seen as a vital step in helping parents to understand the value of the arts process as well as the product. This was felt to be particularly important in some pre-school settings where there was an expectation of 'taking something home' at the end of a session.

Parental self-expression

Developing the arts with young children can also provide opportunities for parents themselves to experience different artforms. Involving parents was seen as important for their own self-expression and as another way of promoting understanding about the activities in which their children were participating.

> Parents need the opportunity to experience the creative process – not the end product.
>
> Early years professional
>
> Its exciting to see a shift in parents' own understanding. In non-threatening environments, deprived families can be helped to learn in a non-academic, non-formal way.
>
> Arts Education Officer

Impact on the wider community

Participants discussed examples where arts-based work with young children had had an influence beyond the boundaries of an early years setting. In some instances, the status of young children, as well as that of the arts, had been raised by taking both into a new environment. The following example describes a celebration to mark the end of an arts project which had involved a network of schools, including a nursery.

> We did a presentation for all the local community people who had been involved in setting up the project in the first place. We had Year 10s in a secondary school as well, but the nursery children all came and presented

their work as part of it. For the local councillors and all these local organisations to see three and four year-olds presenting their work was a revelation.

> Arts Education Officer

2.3 What are the benefits for early years professionals?

The benefits for early years professionals described by participants in the focus groups and case studies included:

- inspiration
- challenge
- self-fulfilment

but access to these benefits could be limited.

Training for early years professionals was ranked as a 'very important' aim for the arts and early years by 57% of the questionnaire respondents.

Inspiration

Collaboration with artists may be one of the few opportunities early years professionals have to see another professional engage with the children in their group. The artist may introduce a different approach to communicating with the children. This in turn may lead to new insights into individual children's abilities.

> It adds an extra dimension to teaching.
>
> Artist

Challenge

Participants discussed the professional challenges that artists may introduce. Risk-taking is one such element. Participants discussed moving away from prescribed ways of working, with agreed outcomes, rather than compromising safety issues.

> Teachers are often afraid of starting an activity they can't control. Working with an artist helps them to realise there are a range of approaches.
>
> Arts Education Officer

Self-fulfilment

Early years participants discussed how involvement in the arts with young children had enabled them to re-engage with the original reasons for joining their profession. There was a perception that the ability to work creatively with young children had become lost in the target-driven emphasis of recent years.

> For the practitioners who had become a little stale, it was the way to become much more alive and enriched and to improve on their own practice.
>
> Early years practitioner

Participants were aware that these benefits were rarely available to some groups of early years providers. Two groups were mentioned as receiving fewer opportunities to engage in arts activity and, in particular, to work with artists. One group was childminders; the second, pre-schools and playgroups. Both groups demonstrate the organisational problems involved in artists working with very small groups of children. Participants reported that funding was difficult to find for arts activities in these settings.

2.4 What are the benefits for artists and arts organisations?

The benefits for artists and arts organisations described by participants in the focus groups and case studies included:

- a current and future audience and employment
- inspiration
- challenge

'Training opportunities for artists' was ranked as a 'very important' aim for the arts and early years by 37% of the questionnaire respondents.

Current and future audiences and employment

Participants from arts organisations described how, at a practical level, working with young children provides artists with employment and 'current' audiences. These audiences may include parents and carers as well as young children, thus enlarging audience numbers and opening up new sections of communities to the professional arts. This in turn may build future audiences.

> Its about sustainability – theatre companies are struggling to survive.
>
> Arts Education Officer
>
> Early years experiences can sustain interest into adolescence.
>
> Arts Education Officer

Inspiration

Artists discussed how working with young children had added a new dimension to their own practice.

> It puts you back in touch with your own creativity.
>
> Arts organisation representative

This is similar to the benefit experienced by some early years professionals, discussed above.

Challenge

Participants discussed the link between inspiration and challenge and their own practice. Some thought there was a perception among some artists that working with young children would require a 'dumbing down' of their practice. However, there was evidence that these fears were unfounded.

> I think that some of the artists were a bit afraid that the children wouldn't be able to engage for long enough, to feel that they were developing anything. I think that one of the surprises has been the length of time that some children were able and willing to spend on a project, so that they would stay at an activity for something up to two hours, which is incredible.
>
> Arts Education Officer

2.5 Discussion and conclusion

The views expressed in this study reveal a strong belief in the value of the arts in the early years. Raising self-esteem was seen as one of the most important aims, which in turn is linked to increasing communication skills. Some powerful examples have been shared where involvement in an arts activity has been the key to a child speaking in an early years setting for the first time. These breakthroughs can be of great significance for the individual children, parents and practitioners involved. Confidence gained can enable the children to become more actively engaged not just in the arts but in learning and living in the early years setting.

The cultural dimension of developing the arts with young children is also important. It too is linked to self-esteem, where young children's self-identity can be strengthened and celebrated through the arts.

An artist photographed individual children in their Eid clothes, surrounded by special personal items they had brought from home. Colour photocopies were made of these photographs, which were then transferred to acetate to use with a lightbox.

Case Study Four

This process, however, deserves more study. What is it about the arts which can cause children to leap forward? How significant are the partnerships between early years practitioners and the wider arts community in this respect? There are suggestions from the study that one of the benefits for early years practitioners of working with artists is the exposure to different pedagogues or approaches to learning. These will differ from artist to artist and, to some extent, according to artforms. Opportunities to see another adult engage with a group of children they know well are often rare for an early years practitioner. Opportunities to observe other professionals in this way can lead to changes in teaching styles as well as to new understandings of individual children's competencies.

Changing expectations can also apply to parents as well. Participants discussed examples where parents had been surprised at what their young children could achieve through the arts. This also applied in some cases to parents' perception of their own abilities where they had enjoyed being part of the learning experience. Artists and arts organisations clearly have the potential to help create informal learning environments, especially in communities where formal education is not associated with success.

A wide range of benefits for young children, artists, parents and practitioners has been identified. How can this area of work be documented and evaluated? This discussion is part of a wider debate in the arts community about how to 'measure the magic' (Hooper-Greenhill, 2000). Early years education has a particular model to offer. In the pre-schools of Reggio Emilia, the process of learning is documented through photographs, comments from the children, drawings and video recording. The visibility and openness of this approach, together with the emphasis on process, suggests it may be of value in considering models of evaluation for the arts. Similarly, Woolf (2000) offers an interesting model for the self-evaluation of arts education work.

What messages emerged from the discussions about the early years curriculum and the arts? Participants discussed how using the arts need not be in conflict with the early learning goals: they provide a vehicle for exploring every area of the curriculum. However, anxieties were expressed about the pressure in schools from a 'measurement culture' where achievable targets are paramount. This theme will be explored in more detail in the following sections.

Participants were keen to protect young children's right to play.

> I think it is important that as an artist and as a human being and as a child that you are put in situations in which you can feel free to play and let your imagination roam and create. It is often from that sensation that you then want to acquire the techniques to express yourself better, or to take your exploration further.

> Artist

The importance of play is supported in the QCA curriculum guidance, including the value of play 'to explore, develop and represent learning experiences which help [children] make sense of their world' (QCA 2000; 25).

The wide range of benefits for young children in engaging in the arts hinges on the question of training and the training needs of both arts and early years practitioners. There was an acknowledgement that young children might experience a very prescriptive form of arts-based teaching which was more to do with copying than freedom to express themselves and to experiment.

The arts in the early years

This section has introduced some key issues about the nature of the arts in the early years and has identified possible areas for development. These will be considered in more detail in the following sections, beginning with the structures, staffing and policies for the arts and the early years.

3 Policies, staffing and structure

This section looks at policies about the arts in the early years and at other structures and relationships supporting this work. It considers both the present situation and future plans. These issues are covered under the following sub-headings:

3.1 Policy and staffing. Do organisations have policies on the arts and young children and do they have designated people in post responsible for this area of work?

3.2 Training. Who is providing training for early years practitioners and for artists, and what forms does the training take?

3.3 Networks. Are there specific networks for those interested in arts in the early years?

3.4 Funding. What sources of funding have been used for the arts in the early years?

3.5 Partnerships. Are organisations organising arts activities in collaboration with others?

3.6 Specific plans. What future plans are there for developing the arts in the early years?

3.7 Discussion and conclusion.

This section draws mainly on answers to the survey, including details of key projects identified by respondents as examples of current practice. Focus group discussions and case-study material are also referred to where applicable.

3.1 Policy and staffing

Policy

Respondents were asked: 'Does your organisation have a policy on the arts in the early years?' Less than a quarter of the respondents did (Table 5, below), but the proportion varied according to the type of group. Two-thirds of Early Excellence Centres (EECs) had a policy, in contrast with only one in five of the arts education agencies. The Sure Start programmes were the group of respondents least likely to have a policy.

The arts in the early years

Table 3.1: Percentage of respondents who said their organisation has a policy on arts in the early years

Policy	Number	Percentage
Yes	49	25
No	142	71
Not sure	9	5
Base	**200**	

Note: Rounding up makes the percentage column add up to more than 100 per cent.

Where policies existed, what type of artforms do they cover? Music was the most frequently mentioned artform, closely followed by visual arts and crafts, dance and drama. Media and multi-media were mentioned less often (Table 3.2, below).

Table 3.2: Artforms included in policies for the arts in the early years

Artforms	Number	Percentage
Policy covers music	43	91
Policy covers visual arts and crafts	41	87
Policy covers drama	38	81
Policy covers dance	37	79
Policy covers literature	28	60
Policy covers media and multi-media	19	40
Base	**47**	

Note: Respondents could select more than one of the artforms

Table 3.3: Areas of work covered by arts in the early years policies

Areas Of Work	Number	Percentage
Learning	44	96
Training	35	76
Evaluation	26	57
Research	13	28
Visits	18	39
Base	**46**	

Note: Respondents were able to state more than one areas of work covered

Policies cover a number of areas of early years work. Nearly all respondents with policies include children's learning as a key policy area. The Foundation Stage of the National Curriculum had influenced these respondents in drawing up policies on learning, young children and the arts. Next came training, cited by three-quarters of respondents with an arts and early years policy. However, as discussed in section 3.2, many organisations without a policy have also provided training in the arts in the early years: the absence of a policy does not mean there is no activity in this area.

Staff

Respondents were asked if their organisation has a person designated to develop the arts in the early years. About a quarter said they have (Table 3.4).

Table 3.4: Percentage of respondents whose organisation has a designated person with responsibility for developing arts in the early years

Organisation	Number	Percentage
Those with staff who have a designated responsibility for arts	58	29
Those without staff who have a designated responsibility for arts	140	71
Base	**198**	

Table 3.5: Percentage of each group of respondents who have a designated person with responsibility for developing arts in the early years

Respondent group	Designated Person For Arts in Early Years? Percentage Yes	Designated Person For Arts in Early Years? Percentage No	Base (number)
Sure Start	20	80	25
Education Action Zone	41	59	17
Early Excellence Centre	50	50	22
EYDCP	18	82	55
Local Education Authority	28	72	39
Arts Education Agency	35	65	26
Regional Office	67	33	6
National Children's Organisation	12	87	8
Base			**198**

The arts in the early years

There were illuminating differences between the types of groups. Half of the EECs reported a designated person for the arts, compared with only a fifth of Sure Start programmes and EYDCPs (Table 3.5). This could be because of differences in organisational structure. For example, EECs would be more likely to have a designated member of staff for each of the different areas of the curriculum.

Four of the six Arts Council regional offices responding to the question have a designated person with responsibility for arts in the early years. This contrasts with the arts education agencies, of which only a third (35%) have allocated such responsibility.

3.2 Training

Provision of training

Respondents were asked: 'Has your organisation provided training in the arts and the early years during the past twelve months?'

Table 3.6: Percentage of groups providing training in the arts and early years during the past 12 months

Training	Number	Percentage
Yes	142	71
No	55	28
Not sure	2	1
Base	**199**	

Just over two-thirds of respondents said they had provided training in this area.

The arts in the early years

Table 3.7: Percentage of respondents from each group who have provided training

Type Of Group	Provision of Training Percentage Yes	Provision of Training Percentage No/Not Sure	Base
Sure Start	40	60	25
Education Action Zone	71	29	17
Early Excellence Centre	64	36	22
EYDCP	89	11	55
Local Education Authority	90	10	38
Arts Education Agency	60	40	25
Regional Offices	50	50	8
National Children's Organisations	44	56	9
			199

The organisations most likely to provide training were in the early years sector, with nine out of ten Local Education Authorities (LEAs) and EYDCPs providing training in the arts in the early years. Seventy-one per cent of Education Action Zones (EAZs) also provided training in this area. The role of EAZs in providing opportunities for exchange and debate about the arts is discussed in Section 6.1.

Participants in training

Respondents were also asked to identify who participated in the training. More of the training was for early years professionals than for arts professionals. The need for more training for artists and arts organisations in working with the early years was also raised in the focus group discussions.

Just 28% of training for arts professionals was organised by the arts sector, compared with 72% provided by respondents from the early years sector. Only 11% of training for early years professionals was provided by respondents from the arts sector.

Training and policy

The provision of training was significantly related to having an arts and early years policy. Organisations with a policy were more likely to say that their organisation provided training (Table 3.9).

Table 3.8: Percentage of organisations which have a policy and have provided training

Policy	Training		Base
	Percentage		
	Yes	No	
Organisations with a policy	83	17	46
Organisations not having a policy	66	34	139
			185

Structure of training

The key projects identified by respondents and the case studies both give a more detailed indication of the types of training provided by organisations. These included:

- one-off training events
- projects involving regular training over several months/years
- training for early years practitioners only
- training for artists only
- combined programmes of training

The following examples – a key project and a case study – illustrate this range of training provision.

Sefton EYDCP hosted a conference in October 2001 for early years practitioners on 'Creativity in the Foundation Stage'. The conference included workshops on dance, music, and 2D- and 3D- art. It provided 'hands on' ideas and resources for practitioners.

North West Arts Region

ArtsStart is an early years training project for artists from a range of disciplines and early years practitioners. The artists learned about working with young children and the early years practitioners about the potential and value of involving artists in early education. After the training sessions, each artist was resident for five weeks in one of the early years settings, working alongside the early years practitioners.

Case Study Ten

Training issues raised in the focus groups

Participants from both the arts and early years sectors stressed the importance of training for both groups of professionals. The following issues were raised.

- Concerns about changes to initial teacher training: from September 2002, it was no longer mandatory to offer arts subjects as a subject specialism

    Participants raised the importance of initial training in the arts as well as in-service training. Concern was expressed that there would be less arts expertise to call on within schools if the arts specialism was removed from initial training.

    > Well, before, there was this idea that every primary school would have some arts specialists within it, so that was the mechanism by which standards were kept reasonably high and teachers trained each other in schools.
    >
    > Arts educator

- The need for training in the arts for all early years staff, not only teachers

    Participants were quick to point out that training in the arts needed to encompass the whole range of practitioners working within the early years sector, including nursery nurses and childminders.

- The particular training needs of artists

    Participants raised the training needs of artists. Participants from the arts sector recognised that some artists needed to be made aware of the possibilities of working with young children.

    > There is something to be done around artists working in the early years. Artists not seeing it as the easy option; just because they are little, 'you can do whatever you want'. There needs to be training for these artists.
    >
    > Arts Education Officer

    Participants also raised concerns about the scarcity of training for artists. This was raised in particular by participants from two focus groups: the group in the South West and that for the East England and East Midlands regions.

- Training for OFSTED inspectors in the value of the arts in the early years

    Participants in the focus group which covered the London and Southern & South East regions discussed the importance of training for OFSTED inspectors in the arts in the early years.

3.3 Networks

Membership

Respondents were asked if they belonged to a network of professionals for the arts and early years. Less than a fifth (19%) belonged to such a network. A range of regional networks was mentioned, including: South West Arts Early Years Forum, Bradford Early Years and Creativity Strategy Group, the *Sightlines* initiative (see Case Study One), the *5 x 5 x 5* project in the South West Arts region; West Midlands Arts and Yorkshire Arts. Four national organisations were also mentioned: Early Education, the National Early Years Network, the Kids Club Network and Playtrain. These organisations are not specialist arts organisations but include the arts in their wider brief.

Membership varied somewhat between types of group. Lowest membership by far was among Sure Start programmes, only one of which belonged to an arts and early years network.

It was more common for respondents to belong to an arts education network than a specific network for the arts and young children: forty-three per cent of respondents reported this. These networks included national bodies such as the National Association of Youth Theatres and the National Network for the Arts in Health, as well as regional education networks; for example, the Tees Valley Education Forum.

Networks and training

The key projects identified by respondents and the case studies indicate a relationship between networks and training. There is evidence of initiatives where training has led to the establishment of informal networks supporting development in the arts in the early years.

> Redditch Forum's arts project involved establishing a network of childcare providers, schools, agencies and other professionals. West Midlands Arts funded two workshops for childcare professionals across Redditch, exploring creativity in relation to young children and their learning. Professional artists then visited the early years settings to work with staff and children on various projects.
>
> **West Midlands Arts Region**

> *The Creative Foundation* represents a model of training and reflection for early years practitioners and for artists. The philosophy behind this project supports the development of a reflective community for the exchange of ideas and mutual support. This collaboration includes participating in a series of seminars on 'Building Reflective Practice' and a peer support system of Project Partners.
>
> **Case Study One**

3.4 Funding

Funding sources

About half of the respondents said they had received funding for the arts in the early years in the past twelve months (Table 3.10).

Table 3.9: Percentage of respondents which have received funding for the arts in the early years

Funding	Number	Percentage
Yes	97	50
No	96	50
Base	**193**	

Table 3.10: Percentage of most frequently identified funding sources

Funding Source	Percentage
EYDCP	40
EAZ	28
Sure Start	23
DfES	15
Regional Arts Lottery Programme	14
Trusts and Foundations	14
Single Regeneration Budget	11
Arts Council Regional Offices	11
Beacon schools	8
Excellence in Cities	5
Sponsorship	5
Awards for All Lottery funding	5
Base	**97**

Respondents could name more than one funding source
These figures include external as well as internal funding sources

As Table 3.10 shows, the most frequently mentioned source of funding for arts in the early years projects were the EYCDPs (40%), followed by EAZs and Sure Start programmes. The DfES was the fourth most frequent source of funding, with money coming from the Standards Fund, the grant scheme providing musical instruments for disadvantaged areas, and from support for EECs. Arts funding came from RALP (mentioned by 14% of respondents), Arts Council regional offices (11%) and Awards for All (5%). As relatively few respondents mentioned arts-based funding sources, arts and early years professionals may want to consider how they could access more 'arts' money through the Arts Council regional offices.

The arts in the early years

Table 3.11: Percentage of funding sources accessed by arts and education sector organisations

Type of organisation	RALP	Regional Office	Awards for All	EYDCP	Sure Start	EAZ	Base (number)
Arts Education Agencies	1	3	0	5	5	3	
EYDCP	5	0	2	15	5	4	
EAZs	3	4	0	1	1	12	
EECs	1	2	1	3	0	2	
LEAs	4	1	1	12	4	6	
Sure Start	0	0	1	2	6	0	
National early years organisation	0	1	0	1	1	0	
Total	14	11	5	40	23	28	97

Column totals may not equal the sum of individual percentages because of rounding.

A closer look at the funding sources accessed by respondents confirms that both the arts and the education sectors were more likely to receive funding for work in the early years from education sources than from arts sources.

Sure Start programmes were the least likely education sector group to be accessing arts funding, while EAZs were most successful in attracting arts sector funding.

Funding of case studies

The majority of the case studies had received funding from several different sources. Local authority funding came from counties, unitary authorities and boroughs; contributions were from a variety of budgets, including those for early years and music services.

> *ArtsStart* is an early years training project for artists and early years practitioners. The one-year pilot project was funded by Essex County Council (Early years and Cultural Services), East England Arts, Community Safety Fund and Colchester Borough Council.
>
> **Case Study Ten**

The case studies from the Northern and East England Regional Offices had been successful in gaining funding from RALP. The case study in the London region had received money from the Arts and Young People's Fund distributed by its Arts Council regional office. The case studies in the Yorkshire and East Midlands region had also received funding distributed by their regional office.

Funding from Government initiatives included money from Music Action Zones, Health Action Zones and Sure Start programmes.

> *First Notes* is part of *sound52*, the project of Lincolnshire Youth Music Action Zone, one of twenty Action Zones set up by the National Foundation for Youth Music. The Music Action Zones receive Government funding. The Action Zone is also funded by Lincolnshire EYDCP, Lincolnshire Youth Music Service, East Midlands Arts, soundLINCS, the seven district councils in Lincolnshire and box office sales for a related event. The project has been underwritten by Lincolnshire County Council.
>
> **Case Study Six**

Case studies in the London and East England regions were part-funded by grant-making trusts, one from the Esmée Fairbairn Trust and one from the Clore Duffield Foundation.

> *What is a present*, a cross-artform participatory project, received funding from the Arts and Young People's Fund distributed by London Arts. This was match-funded by the Esmée Fairbairn Trust. These grants were in addition to money used from The Croydon Clocktower's Arts Education budget. Each pupil who took part paid a fee.
>
> **Case Study Three**

Case studies in the Northern, London and East Midlands regions also charged a participation fee to each early years setting which took part.

Case Study Seven, in the West Midlands region, was unusual in relying solely on the use of core funding for arts activities and projects.

3.5 Collaboration

Respondents were asked to say whether the key projects they identified had been carried out in partnership with external organisations. Just under half (45%) of the key projects identified by respondents included funding partnerships. There were collaborations:

- across the early years sector; for example, between private and voluntary early years settings and between a Sure Start programme and an EEC
- between art galleries, libraries and early years settings
- between an EAZ, a theatre company and early years settings
- across phases of education, from nursery to primary to secondary school

The following are two examples of key projects which illustrate the range of collaboration taking place in the arts and early years.

> *Wheels on the Bus* project. Performing arts staff from Woldgate Secondary School and a local sixth form centre have provided a series of workshops for early years practitioners and staff from feeder schools to develop their skills and confidence in using performing arts with children. This is a collaborative project with staff from West Yorkshire Playhouse, Early Years Curriculum Project Managers and local performing arts agencies. Parents have had the opportunity to take part in some of the activities.
>
> **Yorkshire Arts Region**

> *5 x 5 x 5* project. Five pre-schools are working with five artists and five galleries over 12 months, in Bath and North East Somerset. This project is co-ordinated by the EYDCP and has developed from a *5x5x5* project with school-age children. The aims include developing and fostering creativity and innovation in and with young children and transforming practice in early years education by establishing creativity as an essential foundation for learning. The project is based on principles from Reggio Emilia.
>
> **South West Arts Region**

The case studies revealed a range of external partners and collaboration. In some cases the collaboration involved informal contacts; for example, to help with publicity. In other instances, partnerships were more formal. Partners were not necessarily funders.

The arts in the early years

Table 3.12: Case study collaboration

Case Study	Artists	Arts orgs.	EYDCP	Sure Start	Early years settings	LEA & County Council Arts & Early Years Advisers	Other partners
1. Northern Arts	✔	✔				✔	
2. East England Arts			✔	✔		✔	
3. London Arts			✔			✔	
4. Yorkshire Arts	✔	✔				✔	
5. South West Arts		✔	✔	✔			
6. East Midlands Arts		✔	✔			✔	Other partners: Lincs. County Council; seven local authorities; Lincs. Youth Service; Pre-school Learning Alliance; YMCA; LAB Logic records
7. West Midlands Arts	✔		✔			✔	✔ DfES ✔ Warwickshire Arts & Education
8. North West Arts	✔		✔		✔	✔	
9. Southern & South East Arts	✔		✔	✔		✔	✔ Local arts centre
10. East England Arts	✔	✔				✔	✔ East England Arts Conference

3.6 Future plans

Four-fifths of organisations and programmes have specific plans for developing the arts in the early years over the next 12 months (Table 3.13).

Table 3.13: Percentage of respondents who said their organisation has specific plans for developing the arts in the early years

Specific Plans	Number	Percentage
Yes	160	80
No	29	14
Not Sure	12	6
Base	**201**	

These plans include the following activities.

- Training (73%)[2]
- Working with artists (66%)
- Curriculum development (54%)
- Working with partner arts organisations (46%)
- Working with partner early years organisations (41%)
- Special events (38%)
- Policy development (34%)
- Other plans (26%)

Other plans include conducting an audit of arts initiatives within the early years, developing groups for parents and young children which would focus on the arts and holding exhibitions of children's work.

3.7 Discussion and conclusion

The study reveals a complex picture. Responding organisations are involved in a considerable amount of arts work with young children, and most have specific plans for its development. However, only a minority has policies on arts in the early years and designated staff with responsibility for developing this area of work.

There may be a number of reasons for this. It could be because so many of the early years structures are themselves new; structures to support specific areas of work, like the arts, may come in time. Some organisations are not geared up to supporting work in this way. The Sure Start programmes are one such case. The Sure Start Unit publishes targets for each programme's work with families and children. However, the exact methods to be used or curriculum areas to be explored are not mentioned. Sure Start regional managers who responded to the

---

[2] The percentages shown are calculated from the total number of respondents who said their organisation had specific plans

survey explained that specific policies on the arts did not exist, but that support for developing the arts would be given to those individual programmes requesting it.

However, having a policy or designated worker does not seem to be a clear indicator of interest or activity: many organisations without such structures are involved in training and other work and have a knowledge of local arts organisations. The case studies suggest that one of the driving forces behind developing work in the arts in the early years is not having a policy or a named person, but having individuals with an interest in and enthusiasm for promoting such work.

> The Arts Education Officer brought previous experience to the post and was aware of the potential of working with pre-school children on public arts projects. Her enthusiasm and vision were contagious and convinced other people that such a project was possible.
>
> **Case Study Three**

The message seems to be that although it is important to have the structures in place to support long-term development of the arts in the early years, the role of the inspired individual is also important.

Training emerges as an important current and future activity. At present it is being undertaken in varied ways and involves a diversity of trainers. Learning is taking place not only among those receiving training, but also among trainers themselves. How can the accruing knowledge about training in this field be reviewed, evaluated, exchanged and developed?

Training is also a means of sharing experience and disseminating good practice about arts work with young children. Focus group participants identified a lack of training as one of the factors holding back development in this field. There appears to be more of a need for training for artists than for early years practitioners. One reason, discussed in the focus groups, was that many artists needed to understand better how they could work with young children and that working with them can be a rewarding activity.

> It's a message that needs promoting, that working with young children can inform your practice and change your own approach.
>
> Arts Education Officer

At present there is also a sense that, although the arts and early years are increasingly finding ways to collaborate, they are still two different domains, with two different groups of staff – artists and early years workers. In fact, there are increasing examples of hybrids emerging, both organisationally and in terms of workers; the close working over many years of early years professionals and artists in Reggio Emilia has produced 'atelieristas' and arts work is woven into all aspects of early years practice. There is evidence of initiatives in the UK which are experimenting with the merging of boundaries.

> 'We wanted to move away from a delivery model to embedding the artist in the life of the school, as an arts enabler.'
>
> **Project organiser, Case Study One**

Networks are particularly interesting. Although there are a number of formal networks, there is also evidence of the growth of informal networks, stimulated by projects and other activities. This process of connection is productive and begs many questions. What is the longer-term history of such networks? How do they work and what do they do? What conditions enable networks to be creative? What happens if and when they are formalised? There is perhaps also a need for a better understanding of the potential benefits of such networks and how organisations can best engage with them.

Funding for arts in the early years work has increased in recent years, reflecting new policy priorities for education in general, and early years services in particular. But the funding of arts work is often complex, depending on several sources. As in other areas of early years work, this raises questions about the problems associated with multiple funding, including the time spent raising money from different sources and the need to balance funders' differing agendas. There are also clear implications for the sustainability of work over the medium to long term.

These issues relating to policy, training and funding will be raised again in Section 6: National priorities. The report now examines current practice in the arts and early years.

4 Practice in the arts in the early years

This section focuses on current practice in the arts and the early years. It considers the details of the provision looking at the artforms, target age groups, the setting for the activity and professionals' knowledge of the wider arts context. These issues are considered under the following sub-headings:

4.1 Key projects. What examples of current practice did respondents provide?

4.2 Artforms explored. What artforms have been included in the arts work with children in the early years?

4.3 Groups involved. What types of groups have been involved?

4.4 Providers of the activities. What types of individuals or organisations have been involved in the provision of arts activities for the early years?

4.5 Settings for the activities. What types of venue have been used?

4.6 Knowledge about the wider arts context. How aware are early years providers of arts organisations in their local area?

4.7 Discussion and conclusion

Each theme begins with the views expressed by survey respondents. Respondents give an overview of their practice, followed by specific examples of key projects in which they have been engaged. Information from the case studies and focus groups is used to illustrate different aspects of current practice.

4.1 Key projects

Respondents were asked to describe one or two key arts in the early years projects or initiatives in which their organisation had been involved. One hundred and eighteen respondents (58%) described either one or two projects or initiatives, giving a total of 164 projects.

Table 4.1 gives examples of the diversity of arts projects for young children about which we received information.

Table 4.1: Examples of the types of key projects

Key Project	Type of project	Partners involved	Participants
Artforms	Jewellery- making with nationally-known jeweller	Sure Start, EAZ and a local primary school	Children 3-6 years Parents
Artist in residence	Artist in residence in an EEC. Artform: dance	Arts organisation	Birth to 3 Children 3-6 years Parents Early years staff Artists
Networks	EAZ creativity working group	EAZ staff across all education sectors including EEC	Education staff
Special events	Visit from theatre company to local nurseries in Sure Start area	Arts organisation Sure Start	Birth to 3 Children 3-6 years Parents
Galleries	Early years gallery partnership linked to National Children's Art Day	City art gallery 6 early years settings visual artist	Children 2-6 years Parents Early years staff & mentor staff Artists

Respondents were asked to describe their organisation's involvement with the projects. Details were given for 158 of the projects.

- 83 (52%) of those who identified key projects were the funders or joint-funders of those projects
- 89 (56%) were themselves the main organisers of the projects
- 71 (45%) were partners in the project with an external organisation

4.2 Artforms explored

Overview

Respondents were asked to identify the artforms used in their work with young children.

The four main artforms featuring in arts activity with young children were music, visual arts, dance and drama. Almost three quarters of respondents (71%) identified music as one of the artforms included in work with young children, followed by visual arts and crafts (68%). Literature and media/multi-media were mentioned less frequently.

The arts in the early years

This pattern is reflected in the information gained about policies and artforms (see Section 3.1) where literature and media or multi-media were less likely to feature in arts policies. Other artforms described in the policies included puppetry and design and technology.

Key projects

An analysis of the artforms used in the key projects identified a similar use of music as in the general overview (above).

Respondents provided details for 159 of the projects.

- 111 (70%) identified music as being involved in the key project

Projects in which music was the main artform ranged from county-wide initiatives (see Case Study Six) to sessions in individual pre-school settings. There were a number of music sessions for babies and parents. Several projects were supported by the National Foundation for Youth Music's First Steps programme, which is designed for 'children 0-5' and includes ante-natal classes for mothers and their partners.

> A research project, *First Steps*, in partnership with the University of Northumbria is looking at the importance of music for early years development – musicians are placed in nurseries to work together with children, parents and staff to develop different aspects of music-making.
>
> **Northern Arts**

- 96 (60%) identified the visual arts and crafts

Projects involving the visual arts and crafts included large-scale painting, collage, mosaics, weaving and sculpture. There were a number of initiatives where a visual artist was engaged with young children as part of a regeneration project, creating murals and changing their immediate environment in other ways. Visual artists were also involved in residencies in early years settings, including playgroups and parent and toddler groups.

> *Go Wild Outdoors* was a cross-curricular project linking a special school and a primary school by creating a sculpture trail together.
>
> **South West Arts**

- 80 (50%) identified dance as one of the artforms involved

The majority of the dance initiatives combined music and dance (see Case Study Five). There was also a cultural diversity dimension to some of the dance-based activities; for example, enabling young children to experience Asian or African dance.

The arts in the early years

> A babies' dance session was held in a dance studio and was linked to a variety of creative arts activities for the members of a local childminding group.
>
> **North West Arts**

- 71 (45%) identified drama as involved in the key projects

Drama was often combined in the projects with music and dance. There were examples where regional theatres were part of projects to promote the arts in the early years, e.g. Nottingham Playhouse, West Yorkshire Playhouse and The Mercury Theatre, Colchester (see Case Study Ten).

> Eight role-play areas were set up at Thatcham Discovery Centre (an environmental centre) linked to the external environment and focused on the literacy and numeracy opportunities of role-play.
>
> **Southern & South East Arts**

- 48 (30%) identified literature as one of the artforms involved

Although literature was only part of about one in three projects described, there were some innovative examples of integrating literature with other arts activities (see Case Study Nine). There were several examples of encouraging children's storytelling or story-building through work with artists. Several projects involved older children working with younger children, and some involved partnerships with libraries.

> Year 6 pupils (10-11 year olds) were trained to listen to young children in a nursery, encouraging the younger children in storytelling and story-acting.
>
> **London Arts**

- 37 (23%) identified media or multi-media activities

Less than one in four key projects involved the use of media or multi-media techniques. There were examples where photography and light boxes have been used successfully with young children (see Case Study Four).

> Artists ran workshops in a nursery on light and colour which led to the creation of animated projections. These were presented as part of a major public multi-media event: the Acton Crawl.
>
> **London Arts**

The majority of the projects, including the examples above, did not involve only a single artform. Three-quarters of the key projects identified involved a combination of artforms.

The arts in the early years

> Three to seven year olds were involved in a cross-artform project at The Croydon Clocktower. They had the opportunity to participate in a variety of arts activities around the theme of presents and giving. The artforms included music, dance and the visual arts. Artists incorporated the children's work into a large-scale installation based on the idea of presents for the building. The children then returned to the Clocktower to see the final installation and to meet a storyteller.
>
> **Case Study Three**

There were some notable differences between the types of group and the artforms used in the key projects.

Table 4.2: Artforms included in the key projects by type of organisation

Organisation	Artforms used in key projects (Number)						
	Music	Dance	Drama	Visual arts	Lit.	Media	Base
Arts Education Agency	18	15	14	15	7	4	24
Early Excellence Centre	10	10	4	13	6	7	24
Sure Start	18	13	11	4	7	4	21
Education Action Zone	6	9	11	9	6	6	16
Total							85

Key projects described by Sure Start programmes were more likely to include music (86%) than those described by other types of organisation. These projects were also less likely to involve the visual arts, with less than a fifth (19%) of projects doing so. Only one of the key projects involved five or more artforms.

Key projects described by respondents from EAZs involved the most frequent use of drama (69%) as compared to EECs where only one in six (15%) involved drama. The impact of EAZs on current arts practice in the early years will be discussed below (4.7).

Arts education agencies displayed a more even use of music, dance, drama and visual arts. This group was also more likely than the others to support projects which involved a range of artforms. One in four of these key projects involved five or more artforms.

The arts in the early years

4.3 Participants

Overview

Respondents were asked: 'for which of the following groups has your organisation arranged arts activities over the past twelve months?'

Table 4.3: Participants in arts activities

Participants	Number	Percentage
3 to 6 year olds	127	62
Birth to 3 year olds	74	36
Parents and carers	67	33
Other	11	5
Not sure	10	5
Base	**204**	

Note: Respondents could state more than one group

Almost two-thirds of respondents had run arts activities for young children aged three to six, whereas only a third were working in the arts with the under threes. However, just under half of the key projects involved these youngest children (see below).

One in three respondents also provided activities for parents and carers and over half of the key projects involved parents in some way.

Table 4.4: Participants in arts activities, by type of organisation or programme

Type of organisation or programme	Birth to 3 years	3 to 6 years	Parent/ carers	Other	Base
	Percentage				
Sure Start	92	65	61	11	26
Education Action Zone	19	81	31	6	16
Early Excellence Centre	78	100	61	9	23
EYDCP	25	55	25	4	51
Local Education Authority	19	64	22	0	36
Arts Education Agency	24	76	32	8	25
Total					**177**

Note: Respondents could state more than one group

Arts education agencies named children aged between three and six as the target group in four out of five cases.

The arts in the early years

Early years organisations were engaged in more activities with the youngest children, from birth to three years, than arts education agencies. The majority (78%) of EECs, for example, identified arts-related work with birth to three year olds, while just a quarter of the arts education agencies were working with this younger age group.

Respondents from Sure Start programmes, whose remit is to work with children under four and their families, identified work with children from birth to three in almost all (92%) of cases. Together with the EECs, Sure Start programmes were most likely to include parents in activities.

Key projects

The majority of projects involved children aged between three and six years. Respondents gave details for 160 of the projects.

- Four-fifths of the key projects involved children aged between three and six years: 129 projects (81%)

The projects included children in a wide range of early years settings, including playgroups, nursery schools, children in reception classes and those attending after school clubs.

- There were fewer projects involving children from birth to three: 79 projects (49%)

This group also included children 'pre-birth', in ante-natal classes.

- Parents or carers participated in half of the projects: 85 projects (53%)

The involvement of parents ranged from supporting their young children in arts activities to taking part in additional arts sessions arranged for parents. One respondent commented:

> An exhilarating project for everyone – allowed parents to join in and surprise themselves, especially those who never go into school.

4.4 Providers of the activities

Overview

Respondents were asked to specify which individuals/organisations had been involved in their organisation's delivery of arts activities for the early years during the past 12 months.

Respondents could state more than one organisation or individual as a provider.

Table 4.5: Individuals/organisations used as providers by type of organisation or programme

Types Of Group	Early years Staff	Artists	Arts organisations	Base
	Percentage			
Sure Start	80	52	44	25
Education Action Zone	56	75	56	16
Early Excellence Centre	91	61	39	23
EYDCP	86	56	32	50
Local Education Authority	86	68	35	37
Arts Education Agency	44	68	48	25
Arts Council Regional Office	13	13	37	8
National children's charities/early years organisations	33	25	8	9
Total				193

Note: Respondents could state more than one provider

EYDCPs and Sure Start programmes identified early years professionals as providers in four out of five cases.

Only half of the Sure Start programmes (52%) referred to an artist being the provider of arts work. In contrast, three out of four respondents from EAZs had worked with professional artists. Research with a larger sample of EAZs and Sure Start programmes would show whether these patterns are echoed across these Government initiatives.

Key projects

There were some interesting differences between the overview given by respondents about providers and the details they gave about key projects.

- 124 (76%) of respondents to this question listed early years professionals as being involved in the key projects
- 121 (75%) identified professional artists as being involved in project delivery
- 82 (51%) of respondents also named arts organisations as being involved

A higher number of professional artists were involved in the key projects than stated in the general overview. This suggests that partnerships with artists were more likely to occur in discrete projects than in ongoing, integrated work with young children in the early years.

The arts in the early years

4.5 Settings for the activities

Respondents were asked to specify the different types of venue used by their organisation for arts work with young children over the past 12 months.

Table 4.6: Venues used by respondents for arts provision

Venues used for arts provision	Number	Percentage
School	110	54
Other Venues	71	35
Curriculum Development Centre	50	24
Outdoor Environment	41	20
Library	36	18
Gallery	35	17
Theatre	31	15
Museum	21	10
Leisure Centre	18	9
Not Sure	11	5
Base	**204**	

Note: Respondents could state more than one venue

Schools were the most mentioned venues, used by nearly two-thirds of respondents. The high number of 'other venues' included playgroups, EECs and nurseries (35 responses), and arts centres, conference facilities, hospitals and baby clinics.

The arts in the early years

Table 4.7: The use of schools, curriculum development centres and libraries as venues for arts provision by type of organisation

Types Of Organisation	Schools	Curriculum Development Centres	Libraries	Base (number)
	\multicolumn{3}{c}{Percentage}	
Sure Start	27	4	23	26
Education Action Zone	93	7	7	14
Early Excellence Centre	78	22	22	23
EYDCP	56	37	21	48
Local Education Authority	78	56	19	37
Arts Education Agency	59	18	13	22
Arts Council Regional Office	25	0	0	8
National children's charities/early years organisations	11	0	0	9
Total				187

Note: Respondents could state more than one group

The pattern of usage varied between types of group. Education Action Zones made the highest use (93%) of schools as a setting for arts activities. This compares with Sure Start programmes where only a quarter (27%) of respondents identified schools as a venue. These differences are in keeping with the nature of these groups, as EAZs are school-focused, whereas Sure Start programmes are mainly community-focused.

Similarly, as expected, Curriculum Development Centres (CDCs) were most used by LEAs (78%) and EYDCPs (56%). The CDCs are LEA-run centres for the provision of training for educational professionals.

Sure Start programmes were the most likely to use libraries as a venue. This again emphasises the community nature of the programmes.

Table 4.8: The use of galleries, theatres and museums as venues for arts provision, by type of organisation

Types Of Organisation	Galleries	Theatres	Museums	Base
	Percentage			
Sure Start	4	15	8	26
Education Action Zone	36	43	7	14
Early Excellence Centre	22	17	13	23
EYDCP	19	6	8	48
Local Education Authority	19	19	16	37
Arts Education Agency	18	18	0	22
Arts Council Regional Office	25	37	25	8
National children's charities/early years organisations	22	0	11	9
Total				187

Galleries, theatres and museums were used for arts activities with young children by fewer than half of all respondents. Education Action Zones made the highest use of theatres as venues (43%), compared with fewer than one in five EECs (17%). Arts education agencies used galleries and theatres as venues in one in five cases (18%). This compares with their use of schools in almost two-thirds of instances (59%).

A similar pattern emerges concerning the use of galleries as venues. Education Action Zones held activities in galleries in a third of cases (36%) compared with approximately a fifth of EECs (22%), EYDCPs (19%) and LEAs (19%).

However, these figures do not indicate where galleries, theatres and museums have been involved in outreach work in early years settings.

Funding for outreach work has enabled loan crates of interactive displays to be used in early years settings and for artists to work with some of the young children before and after visits to the gallery.

Case Study Two

4.6 Knowledge about the wider arts context

Respondents were questioned about their knowledge of local arts organisations which worked with young children. Over half of the respondents managed to identify at least one local arts organisation (Table 4.10).

Table 4.9: Knowledge of arts organisations working with young children in respondents' local areas

Knowledge of local Arts Organisations	Number	Percentage
Yes	116	58
No	50	25
Not Sure/not applicable	33	17
Base	**199**	

Most of the respondents who said they knew of arts organisations in their local area went on to list one or two organisations, with eight respondents managing to list eight local arts organisations.

Table 4.10: Knowledge of arts organisations working with young children in respondents' local areas, by type of group

Type Of Group	Yes	No/Not Sure	Base
	Percentage		
Sure Start	46	54	24
Education Action Zone	77	23	17
Early Excellence Centre	44	56	23
EYDCP	59	41	53
Local Education Authority	56	44	39
Arts Education Agency	73	27	26
Arts Council Regional Offices	100	0	8
National children's charities/early years organisations	22	78	9
Total			**199**

Respondents from the Arts Council regional offices were all aware of arts organisations working with young children in their area. However, only three-quarters (73%) of the arts education agencies expressed this knowledge.

Education Action Zones (77%) were more aware than other groups in the early years sector. Less than half of Sure Start programmes (48%) and EECs (44%) demonstrated this awareness.

There was a significant difference by region, with respondents from the Northern, East Midlands, West Midlands, London and South West regions being more likely to know about local arts organisations than respondents from the North West, East England and the Southern & South East regions.

These figures concentrate on knowledge about arts organisations working with young children. The reasons for the difference in knowledge between regions are not clear. There may be a need for better availability of information about such organisations in some regions or there may be regional differences in the numbers of arts organisations working in the early years.

4.7 Discussion and conclusion

The study reveals an exciting range of current practice involving the arts in the early years. Music, dance, drama and the visual arts emerge as the most frequently used artforms in work with young children. There appears to be a particular emphasis on the role of music. One reason for this may be directly related to Government support for work in this area.

The First Steps grant programme established by the National Foundation for Youth Music appears to have been of particular importance. The programme encourages applications from a range of organisations, including LEAs, EYDCPs and Sure Start programmes, for music-making activities with children up to the age of five. The programme also outlines what is seen as good practice in this area, including the use of appropriate instruments, structured music-making activities, involving parents and how to continue the work after the programme has finished. It is possible that under-represented artforms, such as the visual arts or drama, could be boosted by a similar scheme.

The impact of EAZs on arts work with young children is worthy of note. The early years sector appears to have benefited from area-based initiatives working across the different phases of education. Young children involved in arts activities have experienced a wide range of artforms and partnerships with arts organisations. This issue was discussed in the focus groups.

> Education Action Zones in some areas have taken on board the early years, but not in all. Where it has worked there have been some interesting crossovers between secondary-aged children working with pre-school children on an arts project, but it has not been developed; it is not there in all of those zones.
>
> Artist

Examples from the key projects suggest that there are benefits to be gained on both sides if older children are given the opportunity to be engaged in arts activities with younger children. This particularly appears to be the case when older children in primary or secondary school can exercise their gifts as artists and mentors.

The arts in the early years

These 'crossovers' need to be documented and evaluated to ensure that any advantages do not disappear when EAZs or other area-based initiatives no longer operate.

The position of Sure Start programmes in relation to the arts and the early years appears to differ from that of the EAZs. Sure Start programmes are not at present set up as part of the formal education sector. These programmes have considerable funds at their disposal which could be used for involving young children and their parents in the arts. There may be a need to enable Sure Start programmes to develop a better understanding of how the arts can help deliver their aims.

The focus groups revealed areas of the country - e.g. Bolton - where arts education agencies were working in partnership with local Sure Start programmes, but this was the exception rather than the rule. It is important to consider therefore how arts organisations can make their expertise more widely available to families in Sure Start areas.

Access to arts provision remains an important issue for the early years, as well as for other sectors of society. The difficulties of accessing arts activities in rural areas are more acute in the early years sector because of the transport needs of young children. There were examples in the key projects of schemes which specifically focused on providing music specialists in rural early years settings.

> *First Notes* is an early years music programme which will operate across a whole county including many rural locations
>
> **Case Study Six**

Focus group discussions also raised the lack of arts provision for young children in some suburban areas, suggesting a more complex picture than a rural/urban divide. Gaining access to the arts is not only difficult for geographical reasons. Access may be difficult for certain types of childcare provision (Godfrey, 2001). For example, a lack of resources may prevent children in a small voluntary pre-school group from working with an arts organisation. There are particular issues of access for children who are placed with childminders, as childminders work in their own homes. The Government scheme, 'Children Come First Childminding Networks', which provides a formal network for accredited childminders, may provide new opportunities for developing the arts with childminders and the children in their care.

Discussions about current practice are given a more in-depth focus in the next section which provides an overview of the ten regional case studies.

The arts in the early years

5   Case studies

The ten case studies demonstrate a range of opportunities for arts activity with young children (Table 5.1). Each of them is described in detail in Appendix Three. This chapter focuses on the messages the case studies provide about how projects like this can best succeed. The selection criteria (as described in Section 2) were as follows:

- Projects involving different partnerships between the arts and early years sectors
- Projects taking place in a range of arts and early years settings
- A range of geographical locations, including inner city, small town, rural and coastal locations
- A variety of artforms
- A range of project types to include artist residencies, training, conferences and workshops
- Projects involving children as audience as well as in 'hands-on' activities
- Projects promoting cultural diversity and inclusion

5.1   Background and inspiration

These case studies indicate the importance of building on innovative practice in the field and adapting these models for new situations. The Start exhibition for young children at the Walsall Museum and Art Gallery, and the subsequent opening of the Discovery Gallery at the New Art Gallery, Walsall have both influenced the development of new practice in this area. The Start exhibition held in 1995 was the first interactive art gallery experience specifically designed for pre-school children.

The inspiration of the philosophy developed in the pre-schools of Reggio Emilia has provided a starting point for several of the case studies. This well-publicised international example has provided a framework for developing practice in this country.

Table 5.1: Ten case studies listed by region

Case Study	Region	Title	Description
Case Study One	Northern Arts	*Creative Foundation*	Long-term project involving artists, early years staff parents and young children based on Reggio Emilia approach
Case Study Two	East England Arts	*Five Alive*	Interactive gallery project with outreach element
Case Study Three	London Arts	*What is a Present?*	Cross-artform participatory project
Case Study Four	Yorkshire Arts	*Kush Zindagi (Happy Life)*	Visual artist and dance group working with young children and parents
Case Study Five	South West Arts	*A Child's Eye View*	Dance and music partnership involving arts organisation, EYDCP and Sure Start
Case Study Six	East Midlands Arts	*First Notes*	Early years music programme across one county
Case Study Seven	West Midlands Arts	*Artist in Residence*	Placement of artist in EEC over two terms, linked to gallery
Case Study Eight	North West Arts	*Early Years Creative Arts project*	Cross-artform residencies based on collaboration between Early years Advisory Service, EYDCP and Artists in Schools
Case Study Nine	Southern & South East Arts	*Story-telling Tents*	Collaboration with arts organisation and early years settings combining literature and the visual arts
Case Study Ten	East England Arts	*ArtsStart*	Network model of training & residencies for artists and early years staff

5.2 Organisation

One feature of many of these case studies is the provision for sustained thinking and exchange of ideas across the arts and early years sectors. Funding for this 'space to think' is unusual in the early years.

> It is a learning group which is not found elsewhere. …it can provide a sociably critical framework for communities who are exploring and developing ideas and practice.
>
> Project Organiser, Case Study One

The arts in the early years

This reflexive model of training brings together two groups of professionals who are sometimes isolated in their everyday practice. Early years professionals may have few opportunities to exchange ideas, regardless of whether they are working in small or large pre-school settings. This is also the case for many artists and appears to have been one of the benefits for the artists involved in these projects.

5.3 Funding and collaboration

The case studies have been funded from a range of sources including grants from the Arts Council and from Government initiatives, including a Music Action Zone, Health Action Zone and local Sure Start programmes, as well as from more local sources (see Section 3.4 for details).

Case-study participants raised the need for funding for the full length of projects. This would remove the time, effort and uncertainty involved in making annual resubmissions for funding. Participants also recommended that Arts Council regional offices should give early years projects priority status for Regional Arts Lottery Programme (RALP)[3] grants.

Two particular funding needs were seen as important if the impact of arts projects for young children was to be increased and the scope widened: first, funding for outreach work and second, funding for established projects to enable them to mentor new initiatives. Participants referred to the particular funding implications for artists working with young children. Financial support needs to allow for the extra staff numbers required to work with young children and the lengthy preparation time, even if contact time with the children is short.

The case studies demonstrate imaginative collaborations across the early years and arts sectors (see Section 3.5, Table 3.13 and Appendix Three for details).

5.4 Children's role

A central feature of the case studies has been the role of the young children themselves. Children have been active participants whose views and contributions have been valued and celebrated. They have been encouraged to use different means of expression and to develop their imagination. They have had access to a range of materials and tools. The focus has been on the children's experiences and the process, rather than being driven by outcomes. Children have been introduced to different works of art - in exhibitions and literature, for example - and have seen their own and other cultures valued. Several of the case studies have raised the profile of young children as artists in the local or wider community – for example, exhibiting young children's work in public spaces.

These experiences are in keeping with those suggested in the Foundation Stage guidelines for creative development (QCA, 2000: 116) and the influential criteria assembled by the Arts Education Partnership Task Force (1998). This national,

---

[3] The lottery-funded Regional Arts Lottery Programme is replaced by a new Arts Council grants programme in April 2003

The arts in the early years

American task force brought together members of the arts and early years sectors to focus on arts in the early years (Clark and Taylor, 2000.)

> **Well-conceived arts activities:**
>
> - Are balanced between child and adult-initiated activities, reflective and active activities, indoor and out-door activities, and group and individual activities
> - Provide many opportunities for child-initiated action. Children need to make their own choices and see their choices acted upon
> - Are stimulating and contain quality materials for children to use, including a selection of books and arts materials
> - Allow children time to repeat and practice new skills
> - Focus on children's experiences and the process of learning the arts rather than on isolated tasks or performance goals
> - Encourage expression and imagination
> - Are flexible in structure, allow for improvisation and encourage spontaneity
> - Should introduce children to works of art – including performances, exhibitions and literature – of the highest quality that are developmentally appropriate in content and presentation
>
> (Clark and Taylor, 2000)

5.5 Parental involvement

Parental involvement emerges as a strong feature of several of the case studies. The most successful examples are where parents have been drawn to the creative work undertaken by their young children and then allowed quite naturally to become involved.

5.6 Follow up

There is an emphasis within the case studies on embedding work with the arts into everyday early years practice. These case studies have not adopted a 'hit and run' approach to delivering the arts. Artists' expertise has been shared in a way that can lead to changes beyond the life of a project. This emphasises again the link between practice and training.

5.7 Evaluation

There is an acknowledgement among organisers of and participants in the case studies that the arts in the early years is a growing area of work in which progress needs to be documented and evaluated. The impetus is coming less from requirements of funding than from a genuine desire to record the differences made to the lives of young children. These themes provide the starting point for the following section, which focuses on national priorities for developing the arts in the early years.

6 National priorities

This section draws together the views of questionnaire respondents and participants in the focus groups and case studies, all of whom were asked to identify and discuss the national priorities for the arts in the early years.

6.1 Factors encouraging the arts in the early years. What positive factors have led to recent developments in the arts and early years?

6.2 Factors hindering the arts in the early years. What factors have had a negative impact on current practice?

6.3 National priorities. What is the way forward for developing the arts in the early years?

This section begins by looking at the views of focus group participants and links these to issues raised in the case studies. The views of the questionnaire respondents contribute to the subsequent discussion about national priorities.

6.1 Factors encouraging the arts and early years

The following factors were identified by participants in the focus groups and case studies as having encouraged recent developments in the arts and early years.

- New funding opportunities
- Inspirational theory and practice from the UK and abroad
- Exchange and debate
- Structural change
- Curriculum change

New funding opportunities

Focus groups discussed the positive impact of new funding opportunities for work involving young children and the arts. Sure Start, Education Action Zones (EAZs) and Early Excellence Centres (EECs) were singled out as three Government initiatives which are providing new resources for work in this area.

Regeneration initiatives such as New Deal for Communities and the Single Regeneration Budget were mentioned. Some respondents saw EYDCPs as a source of funding, but they were not mentioned in every focus group. Lottery funding was also seen as having a positive impact on developing arts work with young children. However, participants raised concerns about the effect of the increase in short-term initiatives on long-term development (see 6.2).

Inspirational theory and practice from the UK and abroad

Participants discussed sources of inspiration for their practice. The pre-schools of Reggio Emilia were mentioned in each of the focus groups. References were also made to Howard Gardner's work on multiple intelligences. The latter had encouraged some participants to consider using the arts in new ways. Theatre work with young children in other countries, notably Denmark, France, Belgium and the Netherlands, had influenced some practitioners.

Two examples were given of exemplary and influential practice in the UK. One was the Start exhibition at the Walsall Art Gallery, discussed in Case Study Two. The second example was the organisation Learning through Landscapes, which uses the arts as one tool to involve children in changing outdoor environments.

Participants also discussed how individuals with knowledge and enthusiasm for involving young children in the arts had had an impact on artists and early years professionals.

> I think some of the current practice has been affected by some very strong individuals who believe passionately in the provision of excellent art for this age range, certainly in our field of work, theatre.
>
> Artist

Exchange and debate

New opportunities for exchange and debate were seen as another positive factor in bringing about change. Benefits included greater dissemination of good practice and the opportunity to discuss methods of evaluation. Respondents named EAZs as one initiative which had introduced new opportunities for debate and exchange across educational phases, from secondary schools to nurseries. However, not all EAZs included the early years in this way (see Section 4.6).

Structural change

Participants discussed how the creation of EYDCPs had impacted on the arts and the early years. This structural change was seen as a positive move in bringing together providers in the early years sector in a new way which could be used to facilitate greater involvement in the arts. The inclusion of play work in EYDCPs was a particular advantage.

> EYDCPs have now broadened from education to playworkers. Plymouth has play fairs for children and parents and there are opportunities for practitioners to learn about different ways of working.
>
> EYDCP representative

Curriculum change

Focus groups discussed the impact of the QCA Foundation Stage curriculum guidance on the arts. Some participants saw the naming of the creative arts as one of the six areas of learning as a step towards raising the status of the arts within the curriculum. Others from the arts sector believed that the Foundation Stage had created more openings for being involved with the early years than had been the case in the past. However, most participants believed the current educational ethos to be one of the greatest hindrances to developments, and this is discussed below.

6.2 Factors hindering the arts in the early years

Focus group participants saw the following factors as having a negative impact on current practice in the arts and the early years.

- Status of the arts in the early years
- Funding problems
- Training issues
- Structural difficulties
- Educational ethos
- Access problems

Status of the arts in the early years

The low status of the arts for young children was seen as the greatest hindrance to development. Participants saw this as first applying to policies at a ministerial level.

> There are two negatives at the moment. One is that DfES and Government thinking is not geared towards the Foundation Stage and early years; the emphasis is more on Key Stage 3 and Key Stage 4. The second is how the arts are marginalised.
>
> EAZ representative

Creative Partnerships was cited as one example of how Government policy on the arts often sidelines the early years.

Participants also described how the low status of the arts at a policy level was also mirrored by widely-held views among schools, parents and society at large.

> There is still the view that the arts are a hobby.
>
> Arts Education Officer

Funding problems

Participants expressed concerns about the trend towards funding the arts through fragmented special initiatives rather than core funding. Fears were expressed that this could lead to patchy provision. There were particular funding difficulties for the non-maintained sector. There may be more potential funding streams available but there has also been an increase in the time needed to fill in applications and take advantage of these opportunities. The EYDCPs were seen as potential funders, but there did not appear to be a uniform policy across all EYDCPs.

> There is the money there (in EYDCPs) but it depends who is managing it as to whether you get the money or not.
>
> Arts Education Officer

Concerns were also expressed at the cost of funding an artist for small, non-maintained pre-schools.

Training issues

Participants linked the low status of the arts in the early years to the paucity of training opportunities for artists and early years practitioners. Several participants raised concerns about current changes to initial teacher training: from September 2002, the arts will no longer be an available subject specialism.

One training issue for early years professionals was the need to challenge the notion of 'the artist as expert', encouraging instead early years staff to collaborate with artists and to take on board new ideas themselves.

Training was needed for OFSTED inspectors in the value of the arts. A lack of such training was seen as hindering the development of innovatory practice in the arts with young children.

Structural difficulties

Although the creation of EYDCPs was seen overall to have facilitated more opportunities for the arts with young children, the early years sector was still viewed as fragmented, with a wide range of settings and staff with different skills according to their training and role.

This fragmentation was viewed as a major hindrance to developing universal access to the arts for young children.

> If you want to address every child's entitlement (to the arts) in the early years, you have to include private providers, you have childminders, you have such a mixture.
>
> Early years practitioner

Educational ethos

Participants discussed the impact that the emphasis on reaching targets and measurable outcomes was having on the arts with young children.

> Some teachers are fixated on academic progress. The creative ethos is lost.
>
> LEA representative

> I think one of the biggest factors that hinders progress is that it is hard to judge on an attainment score, which is what so much of today's teaching is about: do you show the graph going up? A lot of the fundamentals of the early years will not show until a child is perhaps in their secondary schooling or even later.
>
> LEA representative

Thus the measuring of short-term outcomes was sometimes seen to be at odds with a consideration of the longer-term benefits for children.

Access problems

Participants raised the problems caused by the lack of universal access to artists and opportunities to experience different artforms. This applied to a range of geographical areas including rural, urban and suburban.

Participants from the South West Arts and East England Arts regions in particular highlighted the need for more trained artists to work in their areas.

Access was also linked to funding issues. Participants gave examples where funding could not be obtained for arts activities for scattered groups of children because of the small numbers involved.

6.3 National priorities

This final section discusses the views of questionnaire respondents and focus group participants on what should be the national priorities for the arts in the early years.

Questionnaire respondents were asked to list up to three priorities for developing the arts in the early years. The issues which emerged have been grouped under the six areas shown in Table 6.1.

Table 6.1: Six areas identified as a national priority for developing the arts in the early years, in descending order

Areas of national priority	Number	Percentage
Collaboration	69	44
Funding	65	41
Raising the status	62	39
Training	59	37
Information and dissemination	35	22
Inclusion and access	30	19
Base	**158**	

Note: Respondents were asked to name up to three priority areas

These six key areas were reiterated in the focus group discussions.

Collaboration

A key priority was supporting collaboration between the arts and the early years sectors. Such collaboration involves funding, training, information-sharing and dissemination.

> Give a mandate to early years and arts organisations to work together. Work through EYDCPs to ensure the above becomes a reality.
>
> Sure Start Programme Manager

Participants pinpointed the need for a mechanism to 'bridge' the arts and early years sectors.

> One needs to know what the other does. There is a lack of communication/information. We started our arts projects without knowing who else is doing a similar thing.
>
> EYDCP representative

EYDCPs were seen as one possible mechanism for directing information between the two sectors. This raised the need for there to be arts representation at the EYDCP meetings. Participants also highlighted the importance of the Arts Council regional offices as a second bridging point between the arts and the early years (see below).

The Creative Partnerships initiative was one model for promoting collaboration between the arts and the education sector which could be adapted to work in the early years. Participants also suggested that other models of collaboration were investigated.

> I suggest this project looks at how different agencies can form models of development, which brings in people from different areas.
>
> LEA representative

Funding

Funding was another key national priority. The following funding priorities were identified in the focus groups.

- Core funding of artists' residencies or funding for permanent artists to be employed to work in schools, using the model adopted in the pre-schools of Reggio Emilia
- Funding for the arts across all early years sectors, not only in schools
- Funding to include rural, suburban and urban areas
- Funding to engage more arts officers to work in the early years service
- Support for franchised provision of an agreed curriculum funded through regional or local arts funding
- Funding for initial and ongoing training for artists, early years staff and parents (see below)
- Funding for individual arts events, joint projects - e.g. with theatres and galleries - and access to high-quality venues and performers
- Funding for resources including local swap banks and recycling centres
- Funding for documentation of early years arts practice

The need for both long-term and short-term funding for specific arts events and collaborations was discussed.

> There is no substitute for direct funding. DfES should give money to schools.
>
> Arts Education Officer
>
> I would like to point out the difference between short-term project funding and core funding to run on-going programmes that grow and develop, which is what my organisation is interested in doing. I want to keep this monthly programme going. I would like to run it more often. I don't know where the funding would come from
>
> National Arts Education Officer

Other respondents were keen that funding was not limited to the maintained sector. Attention was drawn to the need to fund the arts in small, non-maintained early years settings and to include resources and training for all staff.

> There should be training for childminders, playgroups, day nurseries and reception class staff.
>
> National early years representative

Raising the status of the arts in the early years

The need to raise the profile of the arts within the early years curriculum and the National Curriculum was a major concern for those working within both the early years and the arts sectors.

There was also a need to raise the status of the arts for young children among parents.

> Artforms are non-academic, non-threatening - everybody is a success, you cannot fail – parents open up, engage, enjoy themselves.
>
> Early Excellence Centre staff

Parents' attitudes to the arts were also linked to young children's own perceptions of value.

> It goes back to status. It is fundamental to raise the status of the arts in the eyes of children. If they see parents and communities valuing the arts, they will do it.
>
> National early years representative

Training, information and dissemination

Training was considered to be another key national priority. This included training for artists, early years professionals, advisers and parents. There was support for clear training strategies for the arts in EYDCPs. Particular areas for training were identified, many of them in individual artforms:

- dissemination of the Reggio Emilia approach
- dance and movement
- drama
- music
- visual arts
- display techniques

The Reggio Emilia approach was the only particular approach to be mentioned by name by respondents to the questionnaire.

> The inspiring work done in the Italian nurseries in Reggio Emilia needs to be used to develop the arts in the early years.
>
> EYDCP officer

Discussion in the focus groups suggested that there should be more time given to looking at different approaches to work in the arts, including those incorporating Reggio practice and those which evaluate their contributions to young children's learning.

Training was also needed in how to use new resources.

> There was a classic example of a great deal of funding being made available for musical instruments in the early years last summer, but no training to back it up.
>
> Arts Education Officer

Participants expressed the need for more information about artists who are available for work with young children.

> Could there be a telephone line so that if you are a practitioner and you are thinking, 'I would really love to find a storyteller. Where do I start?' I went to the library but they couldn't help me.
>
> Early years practitioner

There were also requests for more general guidance on selecting artists and on issues around quality.

> A quality assurance programme, guiding non-specialists on selecting an artist and distinguishing skills and expertise to help them in appointing and working with artists.
>
> Arts Education Officer

Discussions about current databases raised the particular issue of organising police checks for artists wishing to work with children.

Information-sharing was also seen as a priority for sharing the results of innovative practice. There was a clearly-identified need for infrastructures to support this dissemination.

Inclusion and access

Some respondents used the language of rights, voicing the need for the arts to be seen as a right for all children.

> The importance of the arts as part of every day. The arts are an entitlement, not a treat.
>
> Arts Education Officer

Improving access to the arts was seen as important in all regions and in all parts of the early years sector, particularly the non-maintained sector.

Respondents discussed how arts activities should reflect a range of cultures, particularly those of ethnic minority groups.

6.4 The role of the Arts Council

Participants were asked to identify the particular contribution the Arts Council, at both national and regional level, could make to developing the arts and the early years. There was broad agreement across the focus groups.

Funding

The Arts Council was identified as being a potential provider of longer-term funding for partnerships between arts education agencies and early years settings, for rural areas and for small-scale early years groups.

> Some kind of funding is needed to subsidise specifically the needs of children in small settings…for example, bringing artists or theatre companies in to create projects with just 10 or 20 children
>
> Artist

Funding was also needed for designated individuals with responsibility for the arts and the early years within the Arts Council, at both national and regional level.

Information-sharing and dissemination

The Arts Council was seen as a bridge between arts organisations and the early years sector, although different regional offices had different levels of knowledge about the early years sector.

> As someone working in the funding system – how do we best link funding? I am not sure how to do it – who are the national key people we should talk to? The inhibiting factor is not knowing who to contact.
>
> Regional office representative

The need for national and regional databases of artists with experience of working in the early years sector was discussed. Participants also recommended the publication of a good practice guide and training pack for artists and early years professionals.

Research

Participants discussed the possibility of the Arts Council commissioning research focusing on current early years initiatives, to include an investigation of how to evaluate work in the arts and the early years. One suggested model raised was locally-based action research, co-ordinated by the Arts Council:

> Teachers could enhance their own professional development and understanding, as well as feeding into a bigger picture.
>
> Education Action Zone representative

The arts in the early years

Training

Participants emphasised the role the Arts Council could play in promoting different models of training for artists and early years practitioners. Participants thought a national perspective was important to draw together fragmented examples from across the country and to develop a more co-ordinated approach.

6.5 Discussion and conclusion

This study highlights a number of recent changes which have been the catalyst for innovative practice in the arts in the early years. However, most of these developments have not led to benefits in all early years settings.

Structural changes within the early years sector have made it easier for early years organisations to collaborate with artists. The creation of the EYDCPs has provided new avenues for co-ordinating initiatives between arts and early years professionals. However, the level of interest, knowledge and awareness about the arts in EYDCPs is not uniform across the country.

New funding opportunities from Government initiatives have enabled some interesting projects to take place, but there is concern that this frequently fragmented and short-term approach may not benefit development in the arts in the early years in the long term.

Curriculum changes also appear to have had a contradictory effect. On the one hand the Foundation Stage has made explicit the place of the arts in learning in the early years. On the other hand, the wider educational climate, with a Government emphasis on attainment at Key Stages Two, Three and Four and league tables of school performance, presents an environment in which valuing the role of the arts in learning is more difficult.

Through this study, providers have identified key areas in which they think progress needs to made:

- collaboration between sectors
- funding
- raising status
- training
- dissemination
- inclusion and access

The lynchpin for developments in many of these areas is the Arts Council. Its potential bridging role between the arts and early years sectors could make an impact on several of these key themes, including encouraging collaboration, promoting funding and training opportunities and lastly, dissemination. A number of the regional offices have demonstrated how effective they can be in this role.

The arts in the early years

> East England Arts (formerly Eastern Arts Board) held a conference on 'The Creative Child' in 2000. This brought together early years providers and those working in the arts to share ideas and discuss the development of young children's creativity through the arts. A directory was produced with contact details for both the early years and arts sectors.

> West Midlands Arts commissioned a report, 'Creative Start', to look at current links between artists and early years professionals. This has been produced alongside a directory, *Artists in Early Learning* (2001), which provides information about artists with experience of working in the early years.

> Northern Arts has named the early years as a priority initiative area. This has led to a number of events to promote dialogue between the arts and the early years sectors and to further research in this area. Northern Arts hosted a national conference on developing creativity in the under fives in 1999.

The final section of this report takes up these issues and considers future directions for the arts in the early years.

7 Discussion and future directions

This final section discusses the findings of this study and points to future directions for developing the arts in the early years.

7.1 The role of the arts

7.2 Curriculum balance

7.3 Organisation and policies

7.4 Funding

7.5 Training

7.6 Artforms

7.7 Conclusion

7.1 The role of the arts in the early years

> Offering to children languages with which they are able to express and communicate ideas and feelings.
>
> Arts Education Officer

This study has reported the benefits and opportunities of being involved in the arts for young children, early years professionals, artists and parents, as seen by early years and arts providers.

All those involved in the study have talked of the benefits to young children of being involved in arts activities. The arts give them the freedom to experiment, develop their thinking and communication skills and raise self-esteem. These views support the findings of a series of studies which have documented the work of artists in schools (Gulbenkian Foundation (1982); Department of National Heritage (1996); Arts Council (1997); Sharp and Dust (1997); Manser (1995) and Oddie and Allen (1998)).

Further study is needed to look at the complex range of emerging opportunities for young children to engage in the arts. Artists in residence will be one model; as the case studies have shown there are a growing number of ways in which young children's contact with the arts can be improved.

There is also the call for sustained research to look at the impact of the arts on early learning (Clark and Taylor, 1999; Sharp 2001) and to build on our understanding of the ingredients of a well-conceived arts activity (Task Force on Children's Learning and the Arts: Birth to age eight. Arts Education Partnership, Massachusetts,1998).

This research will need to take account of young children's own perspectives on this topic (Simpson, 2000). There is a small but increasing number of studies which focus on young children's experiences of early years settings (Miller, 1996; Cousins, 1999; Clark and Moss, 2001). Such approaches would contribute to our understanding of young children's experiences of the arts.

Participants in this study have also indicated the benefits to artists of engaging with young children. These have ranged from the pragmatic, in terms of new sources of employment, to artistic challenge and job satisfaction. Artists working in a range of artforms have discussed how working with young children has challenged and inspired their own practice, as well as being satisfying to do.

Developing the arts with young children is linked to the involvement of parents and the community. Respondents have discussed the benefits to parents in terms of their own creativity, communicating with their children and being involved more in their children's learning.

The benefits to early years professionals include a re-engaging with their own creativity. There are the advantages gained by seeing another professional's approach to working with young children. This has been illustrated in the case studies, particularly where the arts activity has had the time and resources built in for early years practitioners and artists to work together and reflect on children's learning and their own and others' practice. It may be useful to consider how work in the arts in the early years can have a wider impact on pedagogy (see 7.2).

Future directions:

- Further research to investigate the benefits of the arts to young children
- Further research to explore the benefits to artists of working with young children and subsequent impact on the development of their artform and arts practice

7.2 Curriculum balance

> Putting the balance back into the Foundation Stage curriculum – away from the landowners of literacy and numeracy.
>
> EYDCP officer

The findings show a great enthusiasm for the arts in the early years across the early years and arts sectors. However, this commitment has been hindered by a number of factors, including the current educational climate. The focus on literacy and numeracy has put pressure on the arts in the early years. The views given by respondents in this research support the findings of a recent study (Galton and MacBeath, 2002) into the primary curriculum which records the shrinkage of the arts: the decline in the curriculum time available for these subjects is matched by a decline in teachers' own sense of creativity' (The Guardian, July 5 2002).

Our study has revealed feelings of inadequate support at a ministerial and policy level for the arts in the early years. One important symptom of this appears to be the low status given to the arts within the curriculum. The arts are seen as a way of helping to achieve other things, rather than being worthy of curriculum time in their own right.

> We know that 'art' understood as spontaneous creative play is what young children naturally do – singing, dancing, drawing and role-playing. We also know that arts engage all the senses and involve a variety of modalities including the kinaesthetic, auditory and visual.
>
> Arts Education Partnership (1998)

There is evidence from our study to show that the arts and artists are being used to rethink pedagogy. The case studies which have adapted models of learning from Reggio Emilia are experimenting with open methods of learning, often involving groups where young children are supported in developing their own ideas. These models present a challenge to the current education climate because they are process, rather than outcomes, driven. Local evaluations suggest that they are developing children's thinking and learning strategies. It would be useful to draw together messages from these local evaluations to inform national practice.

Future directions:

- National recognition of the value of the arts and the early years and reinforcement of the role of the creative arts within the Foundation Stage Curriculum
- Research to be commissioned into national or regional pilots of the Reggio approach

7.3 Policies, structures and staffing

The commitment to the arts in the early years demonstrated by respondents was not well supported by structures, staffing and written policies. Only a quarter of the respondents had a policy on the arts in the early years. There was also a degree of uncertainty as to whether some organisations had a policy for this area or not. Simpson (2000) found that just under half (47%) of the arts organisations she consulted mentioned under fives in their policy statements. (These arts organisations were selected by Simpson because of their stated commitment to working with children under five.)

The creation of EYDCPs has been one structural change which has supported the development of the arts and the early years. However, there appears to be far greater potential for the arts sector to reach the early years sector through EYDCPs than is being utilised at present.

EYDCPs and Arts Council regional offices both have a role to play in enabling better communication within and between both sectors.

The arts in the early years

Future directions:

- Funding for arts specialists in every EYDCP partnership
- Co-ordination between EYDCPs and Arts Council regional offices concerning the arts and the early years
- A member of staff with responsibility for arts education in the early years in each Arts Council regional office
- The dissemination of good practice nationally and especially between the Arts Council regional offices.

7.4 Funding

This study has shown that current practice in the arts in the early years is being supported by new sources of funding, particularly from the education sector, including EYDCPs, Sure Start programmes, EECs and EAZs. This development warrants further research to explore how these changes have influenced the funding of arts work with young children and their access to that activity. Such research would also need to consider the impact of short-term funding on long-term development.

Regional Arts Lottery Programme (RALP) funding had been used for some early years projects but the possibility was raised of a more widespread use of this funding route for the early years.

Future directions:

- Mapping exercise of all Sure Start programmes and Education Action Zones to document the use of the arts and to dissemination good practice
- More widespread use of RALP for projects involving the early years[4]
- More long-term core funding for the arts and the early years

7.5 Training

Training of both artists and early years practitioners is a high priority. It was also an area which some organisations felt committed to developing. A significant number who had provided training over the past twelve months aimed to develop this work in the future. The key projects and case studies have revealed some innovative models of joint training across both sectors. These regional examples have been brought to fruition by the commitment of a few individuals. What is needed now is for national funding to run pilots of these models in other areas, with external evaluators.

Models for training would need to include the possibility of single sector training as well as for joint initiatives. Discussions from a national conference on creativity and the under fives, hosted by Northern Arts, supported the provision of both arrangements for training.

---

[4] RALP is replaced by a new Arts Council funding scheme, which will operate from April 2003

Training packages also need to be linked to new resources for the arts. There is the suggestion that the DfES *Instruments for the under fives in deprived areas* was one initiative where training and funding objectives were not brought together.

Participants also raised concerns about the status of the arts within initial teacher training. Changes to the training will mean there are fewer teachers in school who have an arts subject specialism. The early years sector has unique training needs because of its diverse nature. Training in the arts needs to be considered across the whole sector.

Future directions

- Re-instatement of an arts option within initial teacher training
- Training packages to be linked to new resources in the arts
- Training in the use of the arts across the early years sector to include opportunities for cross-sector exchange with artists
- A national pilot of different training models which bring together artists and early years practitioners

7.6 Artforms

This study shows drama, dance, the visual arts and music to be the four most popular artforms in work with young children. Music had a high profile, particularly in the key projects where the percentage of projects involving music rose to two thirds.

The National Foundation for Youth Music has clearly had an important influence. Other artforms could benefit from this focused approach.

The role of arts education agencies and arts organisations appears to be particularly important in ensuring that young children in different early years settings have the opportunity to be involved in and experience a range of artforms. This study suggests that Sure Start programmes in particular could benefit from a proactive approach from arts organisations working in the visual arts and in drama.

Media and multi-media work appears to be an underdeveloped area with young children.

Future directions:

- A National Foundation for Young Children and the Arts to model the National Foundation for Youth Music.
- More partnerships between Government initiatives - Sure Start in particular - and the arts sector

7.7 Conclusion

This study presents the findings of the first national study to draw current perspectives on the arts in the early years across the arts and early years sectors.

The arts in the early years

It has discussed current practice at a time of structural change within the early years sector and the arts funding system. Participants have outlined the role of the arts in young children's development as well as the benefits to parents, artists and early years professionals.

Policies, staffing, infrastructure and the different types of organisation supporting the arts and the early years have been examined. Specific early years and arts policies were not widespread, but there was a range of training and funding opportunities available. Access to these was not uniform across the country.

The creation of EYDCPs was one factor which was viewed as a potential positive influence on achieving more equal access to the arts in the early years.

The case studies outlined innovative projects involving young children, where the arts encouraged expression and imagination.

Attention has been drawn to the factors which are encouraging development in this important area and also factors which are hindering progress.

This study points to future directions for the arts in the early years in research, funding, training and dissemination.

Areas for development

- Research into the benefits of the arts
- Research into how much arts work with young children is taking place in Sure Start programmes and EAZs
- Pilot schemes using the Reggio Emilia approach
- Exploration of the potential for core funding for the arts in the early years
- Protection of the place of the arts within initial teacher training and reinforcement of the role of the arts in the Foundation Stage
- Models of training for artists and early years professionals
- Promotion of the use of the new Arts Council grants, available from April 2003, for the arts in the early years
- Liaison between EYDCPs and the Arts Council to disseminate good practice between regions and nationally
- Arts specialists in each EYDCP to promote the arts in the early years

8 References

Abbott, L. & Nutbrown, C. (2001). *Experiencing Reggio Emilia-Implications for Pre-School Provision.* Buckingham: Open University.

Arts Council of England (1997). *Leading through Learning.* London: Arts Council of England.

Clark, A. and Moss, P. (2001). *Listening to Young Children: the Mosaic Approach.* London: National Children's Bureau.

Clark, J. (1998). 'When I Grow Up I am Going to be a Draw-er.' *If the Eye Jumps Over the Wall.* Conference proceedings. Northern Arts Early Years Conference. Newcastle-upon-Tyne: Northern Arts.

Cousins, J. (1999). *Listening to Children Aged Four: Time is as Long as it Takes.* London: National Early Years Network.

Department for National Heritage (1996). *Setting the Scene. The Arts and Young People.* London: Department for National Heritage.

Downing, D. (1996). *Artists in Leeds' Schools.* Leeds: City Council Department of Education.

Duffy, B. (1998*). Supporting Creativity and Imagination in the Early Years.* Buckingham: Open University.

Edwards, C., Gardini, L. & Forman, G. (1998). *The Hundred Languages of Children: The Reggio Emilia Approach.* Advanced reflections. Second edition. Greenwich, CT: Ablex Publishing Corporation.

Eisner, E.W. (1986). 'The Role of the Arts in Cognition and Curriculum.' *Journal of Art and Design Education,* no. 5, pp. 1-2, 57-67.

Eisner, E.W. (1998). 'What Do the Arts Teach?' Royal Society of the Arts lecture reproduced in *If the Eye Jumps Over the Wall.* Conference proceedings. Northern Arts Early Years Conference. Newcastle-upon-Tyne: Northern Arts.

Galton, M. & MacBeath, J. (2002). *Impact of Change on the Primary Teacher's Workload.* London: National Union of Teachers.

Gardner, H. (1993). *Frames of Mind: The Theory of Multiple Intelligences.* Second edition. London: Fontana Press.

Godfrey, E. (2001). *Artists in Early Learning.* Birmingham: West Midlands Arts.

Guardian (2002). 'Art and Music Squeezed Out, Report Alleges.' Friday, July 5.

Hooper-Greenhill, E. (2000). 'Measuring Magic: Evaluating Gallery Education' in *Collaboration, Communication and Contemporary Art.* London: Engage.

Manser, S. (1995). *Artists in Residence.* London: London Arts and St Katherine Shadwell Trust.

Miller, J. (1997). *Never Too Young: How Young Children Can Take Responsibility and Make Decisions.* London: National Early Years Network/Save the Children.

Oddie, D. & Allen, G. (1998). *Artists in Schools: A Review.* London: OFSTED.

Perkins, S. (1998). *Seeing, Making, Doing: Creative Development in Early Years Settings.* London: National Early Years Network.

Prentice, R. (2000). 'Creativity: A Reaffirmation of its Role in Early Years Education.' *The Curriculum Journal*, vol. 11, no. 2, Summer 2000.

Qualifications and Curriculum Authority (2000). *Curriculum Guidance for the Foundation Stage.* London: QCA/DfEE.

Redmond, C. (2001). *Creativity and Child Development: Mapping the Northern Region.* A report for the Arts Council of England and Northern Arts.

Robinson, K. (1982). *The Arts in Schools: Principles, Practice and Provision.* London: Gulbenkian Foundation.

Robinson Report (1999). Department for Education and Employment. Department for Culture, Media and Sport. National Advisory Committee on Creative and Cultural Education. *All Our Futures: Creativity, Culture and Education.* London: DfEE.

Sharp, Caroline and Dust, Karen (1997). *Artists in Schools: A Handbook for Teachers and Artists.* Slough: NFER.

Sharp, C. (2001). 'Developing Young Children's Creativity through the Arts: What Does Research Have to Offer?' *National Federation for Educational Research Paper* presented to an invitational seminar. London: 14 February 2001.

Simpson, P. (2000). *Arts Provision for the Under–Fives in England.* Unpublished MA dissertation. Anglia Polytechnic University.

Task Force on Children's Learning and the Arts: Birth to Age Eight and Goldhawk, S., Arts Education Partnership (1998). *Young Children and the Arts: Making Creative Connections.* Massachusetts.

Valentine, M. (1999). *The Reggio Emilia Approach to Early Years Education.* Dundee: Scottish Consultative Council on the Curriculum.

Appendix One - The arts in the early years questionnaire

Background

This section is about your details and those of your organisation.

1. **Your name**
   (Please circle)

   (Dr/Mr/Mrs/Ms) First name ……………………..

   Surname ………………………………….

2. **The name and address of your organisation (in full)**

   Name of organisation

   ……………………………………………………………………………..

   Address

   ………………………………………………………………………………..

   …………………………………………………………………………………

   …………………………………………………………………………………

   …………………………………………………………………………………

   Postcode ……………………………………

   Tel. no. ……………………………………

   Email………………………………………………………………………………

3. **Does your organisation have a designated person with responsibility for developing the arts in the early years?**

   Yes   [ ]

   No   [ ]

The arts in the early years

> We are using the following definitions in this questionnaire:
>
> **the arts**: developing skills, knowledge and understanding in, about and through the arts.
> **early years**: children from birth to six years

Policies about the arts and the early years

In this section we are interested in your organisation's policies about the arts and the early years.

4a. Does your organisation have a policy on the arts in the early years?

Yes [ ]
No [ ]
Not sure [ ]

> **If no or not sure, go to question 6.**
> If yes, answer 4b and 5 first.

4b. Which art forms does the policy cover?
(Please tick all categories which apply)

Dance [ ]
Drama [ ]
Music [ ]
Visual arts and crafts [ ]
Literature [ ]
Media and multimedia [ ]

4c. Which of these areas does the policy cover?
(Please tick all categories which apply)

Learning [ ]
Training [ ]
Evaluation [ ]
Research [ ]
Visits [ ]

The arts in the early years

5a. Has the Foundation Stage (including the early learning goals) influenced your policy on the arts in the early years?

Yes [ ]
No [ ]
Not sure [ ]

If no or not sure, go to question 6.
If yes, answer question 5b first.

5b. Which of these Foundation stage areas are included in your arts policy?
(Tick all that apply)

	Yes	No	Not sure
Creative development			
Personal, social and emotional development			
Communication, language and literacy			
Mathematical development			
Knowledge and understanding of the world			
Physical development			

6a. Has your organisation provided training in the arts and the early years, during the past twelve months?

Yes [ ]
No [ ]
Not sure [ ]

6b. If yes, tick all that apply

Participants	Training delivered by your organisation	Training delivered by external organisation
Arts sector staff		
Early years sector staff		
Other (please specify)		

7. Does your organisation belong to:

a. a network for professionals working in the arts in the early years?

Yes [ ] *please give name of the network(s):*

....

No [ ]
Not sure [ ]

The arts in the early years

b. any other arts education network or forum (not exclusively about the early years)?

Yes [ ] *please give name of the network(s)/forum(s):*

....

No [ ]
Not sure [ ]

8a. Has your organisation received external funding for the arts and the early years in the past twelve months?

Yes [ ]
No [ ]
Not sure [ ]

8b. **If yes, from which of these bodies?**
(Tick all that apply)

Early Years & Childcare Partnerships	[ ]
Sure Start programmes	[ ]
Education Action Zones	[ ]
Beacon Schools	[ ]
Regional Arts Lottery Programme (RALP)	[ ]
Excellence in Cities	[ ]
Excellence in Clusters	[ ]
New Deal for Communities	[ ]
Single Regeneration Budget	[ ]
Awards for All	[ ]
Commercial Sponsorship	[ ]
Trusts and Foundations	[ ]
Other sources *(please name)*	[ ]

....

....

....

9a. Does your organisation have any specific plans for developing the arts and early years over the next 12 months?

Yes   [ ]
No   [ ]
Not sure   [ ]

9b. If yes, which of the following are planned?
(Tick all that apply)

Policy development	[ ]
Curriculum development	[ ]
Training	[ ]
Working with artists	[ ]
Working with partner organisations: with arts organisations	[ ]
Working with partner organisations: with early years organisations	[ ]
Special events e.g. conferences, exhibitions	[ ]
Other plans *(please name up to three areas of work)*	[ ]

- ....
- ....
- ....

The arts in the early years

In this section we are interested in the type of work in the arts which is taking place, who is involved and which venues are being used.

> You may not know about these details. If you don't know or are not sure please answer **not sure** to questions 10 to 14 and then turn over to the next section.

The arts in the early years

10a. Do you know of arts organisations working with young children in your area?

Yes [ ]
No [ ]
Not sure [ ]
Not applicable [ ]

10b. If yes, please name them here.

- ....
- ....
- ....
- ....
- ....
- ....
- ....
- ....

11. Which of the following areas are included in your arts work with children in the early years?
(Tick all that apply)

Dance [ ]
Drama [ ]
Music [ ]
Visual arts and crafts [ ]
Literature [ ]
Media and multimedia [ ]
Not sure [ ]
Other *(please describe)* [ ]

....

12. For which of the following groups has your organisation arranged arts activities over the past twelve months?
(Tick all that apply)

Birth to three year olds [ ]
Three to six year olds [ ]
Parents and carers [ ]
Early years professionals [ ]
None of these [ ]
Not sure [ ]
Other *(please specify)* [ ]

....

The arts in the early years

13. Which of the following individuals and organisations have been Involved in the provision of arts activities for the early years in your organisation during the past twelve months?
(Tick all that apply)

Early years professionals	[ ]
Parents/carers	[ ]
Professional artist(s)	[ ]
Arts organisation(s)	[ ]
None of these	[ ]
Not sure	[ ]
Others *(which groups?)*	[ ]

....

14. What venues, if any, have been used for the arts in the early years in your organisation over the past twelve months?
(Tick all that apply)

School	[ ]
Library	[ ]
Museum	[ ]
Gallery	[ ]
Theatre	[ ]
Curriculum Development Centre	[ ]
Leisure centre	[ ]
Outdoor environment	[ ]
Not sure	[ ]
Other venues *(please describe)*	[ ]

....

The role of the arts in the early years

In this section we are interested in your professional opinion about the role of the arts in the early years.

15a. In your view, which of these aims are important for the arts in the early years?
(Tick all that apply)

	Very important	Important	Not very important	Not important at all
Developing skills in the arts				
Developing knowledge about the arts				
Developing learning through the arts				
Providing fun and celebrating achievement				
Increasing self esteem				
Encouraging creative thinking				
Listening to young children				
Increasing knowledge about the world				
Promoting positive image of the school/the area				
Involving parents & the wider community				
Providing training opportunities for teachers				
Providing training opportunities for artists				

15b. In your view, what other aims are important for the arts in the early years?

....

....

....

....

....

....

16. In your view, how can the arts contribute to young children's learning and development?
(Please list up to three points)

- ....

....

- ....

....

- ....

....

17. In your view, what should be the national priorities for developing the arts for the early years?
(Please list up to three priorities)

- ....

....

- ....

....

The arts in the early years

- ....

Key projects

We are interested in hearing about current or recent practice in which young children are/were engaged in gaining skills in the arts, knowledge about the arts or learning through the arts. As well as enabling us to report on what is happening across the country, this information will help us to choose a small number of case studies to visit. The case studies will be used to explore in more depth some of the issues raised by people responding to the questionnaire and to provide examples of current practice.

There is space to let us know about up to two projects (**questions 18 and 19**).

> Not sure about the details? Please fill in as much or as little information as you can.
> If you don't know about any such projects, please move on to question 20.

18a.   Title of initiative

....

18b.   Brief description of the initiative including aims, if you know them

....

....

....

....

18c.   Is this a current project?   **Yes   [ ]**

Please give approximate start and finish dates:

[/   /   ] to [/   /   ]

or a planned project: **Yes   [ ]**

Please give approximate start and finish dates

[/   /   ] to [/   /   ]

or a past project: **Yes   [ ]**

94

The arts in the early years

Please give approximate start and finish dates

[/ /] to [/ /]

18d. Nature of your organisation's involvement
(Tick all that apply)

Funders or joint funders [ ]
Main organisers [ ]
Partners with external organisation(s) [ ]
Other *(please specify)* [ ]

....

18e. Art forms involved
(Tick all that apply)

Dance [ ]   Literature [ ]
Drama [ ]   Media/multimedia [ ]
Music [ ]
Visual arts &crafts [ ]

18f. Individuals and organisations involved as project providers/deliverers
(Tick all that apply)

Early years professionals [ ]
Parents/carers [ ]
Professional artist(s) [ ]
Arts organisation(s) [ ]
Others *(please specify)* [ ]

....

18g. Project participants
(Tick all that apply)

Birth to three year olds [ ]
Three to six year olds [ ]
Parents/carers [ ]
Early years professionals [ ]
Artists [ ]
Others *(please specify)* [ ]

18h. What is distinctive about this initiative?

....

....

....

The arts in the early years

> If you have another example to give of an arts and early years project please fill in question 19. If not, move on to the last section: question 20.

19a. Title of initiative

……………………………………………………………………………

19b. Brief description of the initiative including aims, if you know them

………………………………………………………………………………………………

………………………………………………………………………………………………

………………………………………………………………………………………………

………………………………………………………………………………………………

19c. Is this a current project: Yes   [   ]

Please give approximate start and finish dates:

[/ /] to [/ /]

or a planned project: Yes   [   ]

Please give approximate start and finish dates:

[/ /] to [/ /]

or a past project: Yes   [   ]

Please give approximate start and finish dates:

[/ /] to [/ /]

19d. Nature of your organisation's involvement
(Tick all that apply)

Funders or joint funders   [   ]
Main organisers   [   ]
Partners with external organisation(s)   [   ]
Other *(please specify)*   [   ]

……………………………………………………………………………………

The arts in the early years

19e. Art forms involved
(Tick all that apply)

Dance	[ ]	Literature	[ ]
Drama	[ ]	Media/multimedia	[ ]
Music	[ ]		
Visual arts & crafts	[ ]		

19f. Individuals and organisations involved as project providers/deliverers
(Tick all that apply)

Early years professionals [ ]
Parents/carers [ ]
Professional artist(s) [ ]
Arts organisation(s) [ ]
Others *(please specify)* [ ]

....

19g. Project participants
(Tick all that apply)

Birth to three year olds [ ]
Three to six year olds [ ]
Parents/carers [ ]
Early years professionals [ ]
Artists [ ]
Others *(please specify)* [ ]

....

19h. What is distinctive about this initiative?

....

....

....

....

....

Future involvement

In this last section we give details of the next stages of this study.

20. **Would you be interested in taking part in a focus group hosted by the Arts Council of England to discuss the role of the arts in the early years? These discussion groups will take place in May 2002 and be held in five Regional Arts Board regions.**

    Yes [ ] contact by email/telephone *(please indicate which you prefer and check your contact details are correct in question 2.)*
    No [ ]

21. **An executive summary of this study will be available on the Arts Council of England's website on completion. Please indicate if you would like to be sent your own copy:**

    Yes [ ] by email

    Yes [ ] by post

22. **The Arts Council of England would like to receive a list of organisations which responded to this survey.**
    Please indicate if you do or do not wish your organisation to be included on this list.

    Yes [ ] please include my organisation on the list of respondents.

    No [ ] please don't include my organisation on the list of respondents.

The arts in the early years

Appendix Two - Focus group participants

We would like to thank the many people who contributed to this study, including the following focus group participants.

Artist, Exeter	Kathy Norris
Artists in Schools, Bolton	Sue Colman
Arts Council of England	Hassina Khan
Association of Professional Theatre for Children and Young People	Tim Webb
Blackpool Borough Council	Sarah Lambert
Bradford Education	Claire Ackroyd
Bury Local Education Authority, Lancashire	Chris Heald
Camborne [Poolo] Redruth (Education Action Zone), Planbury, Cornwall	Gloria Callaway
Canterbury Children's Centre, Bradford	Helen Sims
Chalvey Early Years Centre, Buckinghamshire	Kate Makinson
Cheshire County Council	Gill Lee
Children's Services, North Tyneside	Katie Watson
Chiltern Leisure Trust, Buckinghamshire	Elayne Hughes
City of York Council	Gill Cooper
Clayton Children's Centre, Manchester	Karen Camm
Creative Industries Development Agency (CIDA)	Stephanie Simm
Customs House Arts Centre, South Shields	Pauline Moger
Department for Culture, Media and Sport	Helen Macnamara
Department for Culture, Media and Sport	Margaret Prthergh

The arts in the early years

Department for Education and Skills	Gina Mahn
Devon Artists in School Initiative (DAISI), seconded to South West Regional Office	Zannah Chisholm
Early Education	Diane Rich
Early Years and Childcare Service (Community Development and Lifelong Learning), Bradford	Ros Lilley
Early Years Development and Childcare Partnership (Advisory and Inspection), Chelmsford	Karen Musgrove
Early Years Development and Childcare Partnership, Derby City	Christine Evans
Early Years Development and Childcare Partnership, Peterborough	Susan Cary
Early Years Development and Childcare Partnership, Nottingham	Catherine Smith
East Midlands Regional Office	Hugh James
East Sussex County Council	Elizabeth Raybold
Fortune Park Early Excellence Centre, London	Helen James
Goldsmiths College & London Association of Art & Design Education (LAADE)	Steve Herne
ISAACS Consultants for North West Arts Regional Office	Ruth Churchill
Kernow Education Arts Partnership, Truro	Amanda Harris
London Regional Office	Paula de Santis Smith
Muriel Green Nursery, St Albans Children's Centre	Sally Douglas
National Association for Gallery Education (Engage)	Sharon Trotter
National Foundation for Youth Music	Hopal Romans
Newham Education Action Zone	Andi Smith

The arts in the early years

North Somerset Local Education Authority, Weston-Super-Mare	Tamsin Fearn
Northern Regional Office	Shirley Campbell
Nottingham City Local Education Authority	Caroline Field
Nottingham City Local Education Authority	Barbara Coombs
Plymouth Local Education Authority	Mary McNaughton
Polka Theatre, London	Jo Belloli
Polka Theatre, London	Vicky Ireland
Pre-school Learning Alliance	Sue Harris
Reading Borough Council	Pauline Hamilton
Sightlines Initiative, Newcastle	Elaine Mason
Slough Local Education Authority	Tara Haikonen
Southern & South East Regional Office	Saira Holmes
Suffolk Education Authority	Joan Sellens
Sure Start South Fenland	Lesley Chambers
Sure Start Unit	Sue Lewis
The Croydon Clocktower	Lisa Mead
The Forge, County Durham	Tony Harrington
Truro Nursery School	Sue Oakes
Walsall Local Education Authority	Jo Goodall
Warwickshire Local Education Authority	Vikki Holroyd
West Midlands Regional Office	Emma Quickfall

Appendix Three - The case studies

Case study one

Region:	Northern Arts
The project:	Creative Foundation: supporting young children's creativity
Organisers:	The Sightlines Initiative

What is the project about?

- Supporting children's exploration of 'artistic media' to develop their creative potential
- Artist as enabler
- Ongoing reflective, collaborative practice between artists and early years practitioners
- Focusing on process as paramount rather than product
- Promoting a view of the 'competent child '
- Taking forward ideas developed in the pre-schools of Reggio Emilia in Northern Italy

This is a three-year project which began in September 2001 devised by the Sightlines Initiative which supports creative thinking and practice in early childhood services in North-East England and across the UK. This project includes eight early childhood settings in the North East, working together with artists and each other. The project sets out to provide a strong professional development framework for artists and early years educators. The artists involved include painters, sculptors, storymakers and a drama worker.

Age range and settings

- Birth to three year olds
- Three to six year olds

The children are from eight early childhood settings including daycare provision, nursery schools and nursery classes in South Tyne, North Tyneside and Newcastle.

Artforms

- Dance
- Literature
- Drama
- Media/multi-media
- Music
- Visual arts

The arts in the early years

Background and inspiration

This project builds on earlier programmes organised by Sightlines. The *Young Children's Creative Thinking in Action* project was first run in 1997 to accompany the Reggio Emilia *Hundred Languages of Children* exhibition which was on display in Newcastle. This work developed into a series of collaborative projects between artists and early years settings. *The Fantastic Attic* was a special five-week event which was part of this programme and involved developing a 'creative exploratorium' for pre-school children, in the Great Hall of Newcastle Discovery.

Northern Arts has made work with the under fives an education priority.

Funding

Creative Foundation has received Regional Arts Lottery Programme funding for one year. The organisers will need to reapply for each subsequent year's funding. Each early years setting also contributes a participation fee.

Partnerships and collaboration

The philosophy behind this project supports the development of a reflective community for the exchange of ideas and mutual support across disciplines and within disciplines: multi-disciplinary as well as inter-disciplinary. Collaboration between the organisers, the artists and the early years practitioners is a key element of the project. They all participate in a series of seminars on 'Building Reflective Practice' and there is a peer support system of Project Partners.

Observation

The artist has prepared a tiled cloakroom area with plastic sheets covered in hessian on the floor, paper from the floor to above head height and large trays of red, yellow and blue paint. An array of different rollers and scrappers are on hand. One girl appears in her swimsuit ready for action.

She puts her foot in the red paint and makes prints on the hessian. She then sits down by the wall and prints her foot on the paper. She then chooses a roller and 'dances' with it across the three huge sheets of paper on the walls, stretching as far as she can reach. Three more girls join in. They are giggling as they make squiggly marks with the roller. One girl puts her hands in the tray and makes careful hand prints around the top edge of the paper, watching how the paint spreads. Another discovers that you can scratch marks onto the hand prints and what it feels like to dribble handfuls of paint onto the hessian and spread paint onto your arms and legs.

Extract from observation of artist's session at Helen Gibson Nursery School, Newcastle: exploring the texture of paint with four year olds

The arts in the early years

Reflections on the project by the organisers and other participants

What are the benefits and opportunities for young children?

- Gives the freedom to follow through ideas which might not be possible in a more restricted framework
- Increases children's confidence to pursue their own ideas in the future
- Creates opportunities for group learning
- Provides opportunities to work with an adult in a collaborative way, which is in contrast to a traditional teacher–learner model
- Offers young children the opportunity to see themselves in a different way;

> To recognise themselves as creators and inventors
>
> Artist

What are the benefits and opportunities for early years practitioners?

- Enables a dialogue between artists and early years practitioners
- Offers the opportunity to reflect on their own practice from a different perspective
- Provides new possibilities for developing children's ideas
- Sets out to be a learning process for adults as well as for children
- Encourages change beyond the sessions facilitated by the artists

> It made us take more from the children's interests, rather than imposing on them. It has had an effect on our practice overall.
>
> Head teacher

Benefits and opportunities for artists

- Provides employment opportunities
- Presents an opportunity to explore working with educators rather than as lone deliverers
- Gives a framework for thinking about their own practice
- There is the freedom to explore ideas as they emerge
- There are opportunities to explore the model of 'artist as enabler' and to develop this practice

> It is brilliant working with young children where the focus is on them and not on the product.
>
> Artist

The arts in the early years

Benefits to parents

- Documentation of the project through photographs, videos and written accounts makes the project accessible to parents

Support for similar initiatives in the future

- There should be funding for the full length of the project; should not have to make annual re-submissions
- Need more resources for educators and artists to have time for reflection
- EYDCPs could support such initiatives in other areas
- More strategic links between Arts Council regional offices and LEAs should be encouraged
- There should be funding to enable existing projects to mentor new initiatives in other areas

The Creative Foundation, together with earlier Sightlines projects, represents a particular model of artist as enabler. This project offers an interesting model for training and reflection for early years practitioners and artists which has the potential to be applied in other regions.

Case study two

Region:	East England Arts
The project:	Five Alive
Organisers:	Wolsey Art Gallery, Ipswich and Christchurch Mansion, Ipswich

What is the project about?

- Interactive exhibition of contemporary art for young children
- Artists commissioned to design five specific exhibits relating to five art works in the gallery's permanent collection
- Partnership with local Sure Start programmes
- Information sessions for early years practitioners about the exhibition
- Series of workshops in the gallery and outreach sessions in early years settings

This project aims to bring young children into contact with artists, contemporary art and their local public art gallery. The project is concerned with enabling young children and their parents or carers to experience art in a new way and also to help foster future audiences for the gallery.

The artists were chosen from a national shortlist to design interactive exhibits relating to five pieces of art chosen by the organisers from the Ipswich Borough Council collection. The entire exhibition is a play space, including a **rag rug garden, tent and tunnel** designed by Susan Branner, in response to Anthony Green's painting *Trimming-October*. Neil Hanger has designed **a mound of black and white vinyl blocks** for children to explore, relating to Langlands and Bells *Millbank Penitentiary*. The Keep family has built **a pair of houses made of**

blackboard and perspex, based on the painting *Blackham Road* by David Ryson. There is a **'room' of mirrors** based on one of Bridget Riley's prints and **a sound and lighting interactive piece** inspired by Maggi Hambling's painting, *Champagne Laugh*. Sarah Florence has also designed **activity overalls** for children to try on and a **magnetic jigsaw**. The original works of contemporary art are displayed alongside the commissioned exhibits.

> We wanted it to be an art gallery and not a nursery in an art gallery.... We are deliberately doing what is hard, introducing young children to contemporary art and then making it easier for early years practitioners to make the connections in their own way.
>
> Project organiser

Loan crates are an important element of the outreach part of the project. Each interactive exhibit has been devised to be portable. These will be packed in crates and loaned to early years settings, to enable children to revisit the exhibits in their own environment.

Age range and settings

- Three to five years
- Parents and carers

Children from local nurseries and primary schools visited the gallery during the Summer 2002. Four nurseries in Sure Start areas have been involved, two of them have also taken part in a National Children's Art Day project.

Artforms

- Visual arts
- Media/multi-media

Background and inspiration

The Discovery Gallery at the New Art Gallery, Walsall was one of the inspirations for this project. The *Five Alive* project grew from the success of a pilot project, *K:art,* held in Spring 2000. This was an interactive gallery exhibition attended by children from infant classes, nurseries and playgroups. Experiences gained from running *K:art* led to a longer-term element being built into *Five Alive*. The pilot project revealed the demand for interactive artworks in environments such as schools, playgroups and community centres. This led to the commissioning of interactive exhibits which can be dismantled, put into 'loan crates' and reassembled in venues beyond the exhibition.

Funding

Ipswich Borough Council and the Wolsey Art Gallery received a grant from the Regional Arts Lottery Programme (RALP). The gallery was also successful in

The arts in the early years

gaining additional funding from Sure Start, South East Ipswich and the from the Clore Duffield Foundation for National Children's Art Day.

Partnerships and collaboration

The gallery has developed links with local Sure Start programmes, including liaising with the Sure Start Children's Worker. The successful partnership funding from Sure Start has enabled the project to include a visit by two artists to two Sure Start Playdays and for six Artist Days to take place. The Artist Days involve artists visiting children in nurseries or playgroups in Sure Start areas. The EYDCP, Suffolk LEA Art Adviser (and Essex County Council Arts Officer) have been involved in publicising the project.

Reflections on the project by the organisers and other participants

What are the benefits and opportunities for young children?

- Young children can come to an art gallery and feel at home
- Young children can see original works of art
- Young children can meet contemporary artists and participate in their work
- There is the opportunity to revisit the exhibits in their early years settings through the loan crates

What are the benefits and opportunities for early years practitioners?

- Resources for talking about contemporary art with young children
- Opportunities to participate in training about the arts
- Opportunities to see artists work with young children in their settings and to work collaboratively on covering curriculum areas

What are the benefits and opportunities for artists?

- Opportunity to receive a high-profile public commission
- Chance to introduce new audiences to their work
- Challenge to their own practice: the brief of responding to the artworks in the collection in a way which is accessible to young children
- Opportunities to engage with young children in workshops, rather than working in isolation

What support is needed for similar initiatives in the future?

- Funding for outreach to allow the widest access to the exhibition and related work
- Greater availability of RALP funding for early years projects

This ambitious project has found an imaginative way of bringing contemporary works of art to life for young children. The extension of the exhibition through the creation of loan crates offers the opportunity for young children to extend the experience in their own settings. The partnership with local Sure Start programmes has added an outreach dimension to the project and opened up young children's access to working with artists.

Case study three

Region:	London Arts
The project:	What is a Present?
Organiser:	Lisa Mead, Education Officer, The Croydon Clocktower

What is the project about?

- Enabling young children aged 3-7 the opportunity to be involved in a large-scale, public art experience
- Developing sustainable relationships with local early years providers
- Bringing together a group of diverse artists to help young children produce an exciting site-specific installation
- Raising the profile of arts education work within The Croydon Clocktower and its wider community

What is a present? was a cross-artform participatory project, which took place in November and December 2001. The project focused on the theme of festival and giving, and culminated in a giant installation being assembled in the foyer of the Croydon Clocktower, which houses a museum, gallery, public library, media training courses, cinema and live events space.

During a two-week period, groups of young children were invited to the Clocktower to participate in a variety of arts activities on the theme of presents and giving. The children had the opportunity to work in three different artforms. They made presents for the building. These included composing music for the stairs, making 'darkness' for the lights and vegetables for the pillars to keep them strong. Artists assembled the presents into the giant installation. The children then returned to the Clocktower to see the final piece and to meet a storyteller, who told the children a story created especially for the project. Early years practitioners were involved at each stage of the project, from the initial idea, compiling a resource pack and evaluating the project.

Age range and settings

- Three to seven year olds
- The groups of children came from nursery and reception classes in local primary schools. No groups came from playgroups or pre-schools, although they were invited.

Artforms

- Dance
- Drama
- Music
- Visual arts

- Literature
- Media/multi-media

A number of artists was involved: two dancers with a background in South Asian and contemporary dance, a musician, a poet, a storyteller and two visual/installation artists, one who works in recycled materials and another who is a sculptor.

Background and inspiration

What is a present? was inspired by a participatory project for under-eights, run by Battersea Arts Centre in 1997 and also resulting in an installation. Changes were made to the structure and delivery of the project when it was adapted for the Clocktower. Changes included introducing different artforms at the request of early years practitioners, offering a range of arts activities and most importantly allowing a return visit for the children to listen to the storyteller and to see the final installation.

Funding

The project received funding from the Arts and Young People's Fund distributed by London Arts which was match funded by the Esme Fairbairn Trust. These grants were in addition to money used from the Clocktower's Arts Education budget. There was also a fee charged for each pupil who took part.

Partnerships and collaboration

The project was designed and co-ordinated by the Clocktower's arts education officer. Early years organisations including the EYDCP were contacted about the project and LEA Arts adviser was supportive but there were no formal partners involved.

Reflections on the project by the organisers and other participants

What have been the benefits and opportunities for young children?

- The opportunity to be involved in an arts project in a public space
- Learning new skills in the different artforms and consolidating basic skills in cutting, sticking, drawing and music making
- Working in a different environment and establishing new relationships with a range of adults
- Developing team work skills
- Giving children something to take home from their visit, as well as giving them the chance to see their work contribute to a giant design

The arts in the early years

> Lots of the children were nursery age and they were really excited at being <u>out</u> of the nursery. They had the chance to be doing a wider scope of art, with less limited resources, on a larger scale and were proud of it being in a public space.
>
> Artist

What have been the benefits and opportunities for early years practitioners

- The opportunity to use a local arts resource and establish links for the future
- To be involved in an arts project from the planning stage and to network with other teachers
- To work alongside artists to gain new skills in the various artforms
- The chance to see children demonstrate new competencies, opening up new possibilities for the future

> Teachers found it really exciting to do….something they had not considered you could do with this age group. It stretched their perceptions and they realised the children could do more than they thought.
>
> Project organiser

What have been the benefits and opportunities for artists?

- The opportunity to work with young children in a participatory way in a public space
- To work alongside other artists with expertise of different artforms
- Employment on a high-profile project

> It gave me the opportunity to work in a public space. I usually work with children in private classrooms and then the work becomes public. In this project my classroom was the foyer!
>
> Artist

Support for similar initiatives in the future

- Funding which allows for the extra staff numbers needed to work with younger children and lengthy preparation time even if contact time with young children is short
- More community funding for the arts and young children
- Funding structures which allow artists more time to spend directly with children
- Access to public spaces for participatory artwork with young children
- To work alongside other artists with expertise of different artforms

This project enabled young children to work together with artists on a challenging idea which had a visible impact in an adult-orientated space. Developing the project created opportunities for new collaborations with other council departments as well as establishing external links with early years practitioners.

The arts in the early years

Case study four

Region:	Yorkshire Arts
The project:	Kush Zindagi (Happy Life)
Organisers:	Bradford Artists in Schools

What is the project about?

- Increasing communication between children and their families
- Enabling children to gain confidence, raise self esteem and develop a positive self image
- Providing opportunities for children, parents, practitioners and home school liaison officers to develop creative ideas by working alongside an artist or artists

The project took place between January and March 2002 in three phases and involved a visual artist and a dance group. The project began with the artist individually photographing the children in their special Eid (end of Ramadan) celebration clothes. The children were asked to fill a 'happy bag' with the things they liked to play with at home and any other special personal items. The children helped to arrange their 'happy things' around their photograph on a colour photocopier. The colour pictures were transferred to acetate to use with a lightbox. In the second phase the children made an archway from boxes and chicken wire. The archway was covered with 'modroc' and lavishly decorated with jewels, sequins, flowers and fabrics provided by the parents. The final phase of the project was a celebration of childhood. The dance group Jabadaeo encouraged the children to move spontaneously to music and to respond to rhythms. The activity inspired the artist to make some musical instruments for future use.

Age range and setting

- Three and four year olds
- Parents and carers

The participating children all attended the nursery class of an inner-city primary school in Bradford serving a neighbourhood consisting of families originating mostly from Pakistan. All families are Muslim.

Artforms

- Visual arts
- Dance
- Music

Background

The Artists in Schools programme provides training and support for a number of projects in schools in Bradford and the surrounding area. In 1999, children in a primary school, working in collaboration with Artworks and Artists in Schools, produced an animation film called *Inside Me.* An artist worked with Year 3 children over a number of weeks, gaining their confidence and encouraging them to express their feelings in personal notebooks. This work led to the writing and recording of a collective poem, illustrated by the children working alongside a professional animator. *Inside Me* is being used as a model of good practice to develop five Arts and Health projects in Bradford primary schools over the next three years, as part of the Healthy Families Initiative 2000-2003. These projects (including *Kush Zindagi*) all share four broad objectives: Health – developing emotional literacy (PSHE and Citizenship); Arts – expressing ideas through the arts (Arts and Citizenship); Social – developing links with families and the community; and Literacy – writing (English Curriculum and Literacy Framework).

These Arts and Health projects are the result of a collaboration between Bradford Health and Bradford Education.

Funding

The projects are funded by the local Health Action Zone and Yorkshire Arts.

Collaboration

The *Kush Zindagi* project centred on collaboration between the organisers, the artists and the early years practitioners. There was a strong emphasis on involving parents.

Reflections on the project by the organisers and other participants

Benefits and opportunities for young children

- Allowed each child the opportunity to respond and contribute in an individual way
- Increased children's confidence and sense of creativity
- Encouraged children to co-operate and communicate with each other and with adults involved in the project
- Improved children's concentration and pride in their own work
- Allowed for non-verbal communication
- Helped children with special needs and withdrawn children to become more involved in activities

Benefits and opportunities for early years practitioners

- Inspired the practitioners to become more involved with arts
- Built up their confidence in their own creativity
- Raised practitioners' self-esteem!

This was a wonderful experience for everyone. Projects like this should be an entitlement.

Early years practitioner

The arts in the early years

Benefits and opportunities for artists

- Raised expectations of what young children are able to do
- An inspiration to own creative practice
- Enabled the artist to work with children for several weeks rather than odd days and thus to work in a more in-depth way

Benefits to parents and community

- Contributed to the removal of barriers between school and home as parents were keen to come in and watch or even participate
- Greatly increased parents' involvement in the school
- Parents, siblings and other family members brought in their own 'happy things' and made their own collages
- Many of the art works still take pride of place in families' homes

Support for similar initiatives in the future

- Let practitioners know about good creative practice
- Allow artists and teachers time to develop children's confidence and creativity
- Emphasise the importance of having an expert work alongside children and practitioners
- Increase funding for artists

The project was clearly driven by the enthusiasm of the artist and the early years practitioners. The project's success was particularly remarkable since this was the first time the artist had worked with young children and the first time the early years practitioners had worked with an artist. It inspired them to apply for funding for other arts projects and gave them the confidence to talk about their experiences to others. One of the major benefits for the artist and the practitioners was the overwhelming interest shown by parents.

Case study five

Region:	South West Arts
The project:	A Child's Eye View
Organisers:	Music & Dance Education (MaDE)

What is the project about?

- Developing the thinking and learning of pre-school children 'in' and 'through' the arts
- Exploring children's play in and through the arts
- Developing a 'learning together' philosophy with co-operative planning and discussion involving all participants - children, pre-school educators and arts workers - and aiming to involve parents as much as possible
- Engaging professional arts workers in the delivery of facilitative arts workshops
- Creating time for shared planning and feedback (informally as well as

formally)
- Observing and monitoring children's play in the arts

> **Observation**
>
> The children and the dance artist are joined by the two pre-school leaders. The artist reminds the children that at a previous session they had suggested a pirates' island as the theme for today's session. The children discuss what a pirates' island reminds them of. 'Dolphins', says one child; 'Scary', says another. A discussion follows about what the pirates need to get to the island. The children hold on to a large stretchy elastic and form the shape of a boat. Artist: 'What does this music sound like? Can you hear the waves? What do waves do to a boat?'. The children rock about. The leaders drift a large piece of voile (imprinted with fish, sea horses and whales) over the children who move around outside the 'boat' as waves. Two children, Anna and Peter, also leave the 'boat' to go into the sea. Anna: 'I'm a mermaid'. Peter: 'I'm a dolphin'. The artist sings a pirate song. The children try to join in or mimic the words. James says: 'The boat goes on the rocks'. All the children lie down (at the bottom of the sea). The leaders drag the 'wave' over the children while 'wave music' is played. The pirates are shipwrecked on the island.
>
> The children come up with ideas of what animals live on the island: parrots (flap arms); monkeys (oohoo); elephants (mimic trunk); snakes (wriggle hands). The artist hands out coloured streamers to all children. They walk around waving the streamers while jungle music is being played. The pirates look for treasure, the artist gives a few children coloured bags (treasure). The pirates are tired and go to sleep (the children lie quietly on the floor). End of session.
>
> The children have remained fully engaged for an hour. They still talk about the pirates while sitting in the 'quiet corner'.
>
> Extract from an observation of a dance session at a day centre, involving three and four year olds

Training is built into the project's funding and consists of two days' training a year for artists and pre-school teachers. In addition, an evaluation meeting with arts workers is held each school term.

Age range and settings

- Birth to two year olds
- Three to four year olds

The children attend six early years settings in Lescudjack (Penzance).

Artforms

- Dance
- Music

The arts in the early years

- Visual Arts

Each artist visits one pre-school setting six times. These visits were arranged in one-hour sessions over a six-week period.

Background

MaDE was founded in 1996 by a dancer (Pat Hickman) and a musician (Chris Morgan). MaDE offers music and dance workshops and projects for all ages, from very young children to the elderly, in a wide range of educational and health settings.

A Child's Eye View 2 is the second phase of a project that began in the spring of 2000 and was inspired by the Reggio Emilia philosophy of the child as chief protagonist of his/her learning. Phase1 was an action research study comparing the development of thinking and learning in pre-school children 'in' and 'through' the arts in two different areas of Cornwall: Penzance and Wadebridge. This project consisted of initial training for arts workers in the thinking and learning of pre-school children and the philosophy of the Reggio Emilia pre-schools; weekly workshops in music, dance, verbal and visual art in six pre-school settings and two exhibitions which documented the research and its outcomes.

Following this comparative study, *A Child's Eye View 2* works in all six pre-school settings in Lescudjack (Penzance). MaDE has brought together a team of nine arts workers (3 for dance, 3 for music, 3 for visual arts) who were given a two-day training programme which was also attended by pre-school staff. During the summer term of 2001, the six pre-school settings were invited to choose two artforms to explore. Of the six settings, five chose dance, four chose music and three chose art. Music and dance was the most popular combination (3 settings), art and dance the second most popular (2 settings).

Funding

Phase 1 was funded by Sure Start in Lescudjack, the Arts Council of England National Office and South West Regional Office and Cornwall EYDCP. Phase 2 is being funded by Sure Start alone.

Collaboration

A Child's Eye View 2 is a partnership between the Sure Start Lescudjack programme, Cornwall's EYDCP and Music & Dance Education (MaDE).

Reflections on the project by the organisers and other participants

Benefits and opportunities for young children

- Gives children the opportunity to explore different artforms
- Develops their individual creativity
- Provides opportunities to develop language and social skills
- Encourages and satisfies children's inquisitive tendencies

The arts in the early years

- Enables children to communicate non-verbally
- Helps children with behaviour problems to understand boundaries
- Increases confidence, self-esteem and co-ordination
- Gives children a sense of achievement

Benefits and opportunities for early years practitioners

- Offers an opportunity to learn new techniques or work with new materials
- Provides them with new ideas they can apply themselves
- Makes them realise how much children learn from arts projects

> Arts projects like A Child's Eye View should be part of the curriculum.
>
> Early years practitioner

Benefits and opportunities for artists

- Working with young children is a two-way process; the children learn from the artists and the artists learn from the children
- Artists working with different age groups build up a more holistic picture of children's development
- Artists soon learn that working with young children is great fun
- Working alongside early years practitioners provides artists with the opportunity to learn from them how to manage/facilitate young children

Support for similar initiatives in the future

- Emphasise the importance of arts for young children's development
- Provide strong evidence of benefits of the arts. Make visible the work including the processes as well as the products
- Identify funding for the professional development of artists wishing to work with young children
- Allocate funding to the arts as one of six areas of learning
- Research the benefits of an arts-centred early years curriculum

This project is relatively unusual in that it has incorporated training for artists and practitioners in the funding. High quality evaluation is also carried out at different stages, using a variety of methods, such as photographic and video evidence, parental questionnaires, scrapbooks, observations of specific children and external observers.

Case study six

Region:	East Midlands Arts
The project:	First Notes
Organisers:	soundLINCS (Lincolnshire Music Development Agency)

The arts in the early years

What is the project about?

- Providing young children with early experiences of music as fun
- Fostering an ability and willingness amongst early years practitioners to make music
- Encouraging parents to think about music creativity with their children
- Assisting early years settings in implementing the Early Learning Goals

First Notes is scheduled to start in November 2002 for a period of 20 months. The project targets 301 pre-school settings throughout Lincolnshire, representing half of all early years education settings in the county, involving over 12000 children, parents or carers and pre-school leaders. Many of the settings are situated in isolated rural areas where children have been excluded from music-making opportunities. The project aims at providing the settings with two months of music-making residencies as well as training for pre-school practitioners and parents. At the end of each residency, an integrated performance by the children and their parents/carers (*Mini Melt*) will be organised. The settings will also be given a resource pack so that practitioners and parents can continue to make music with the children. An independent evaluator will be contracted to evaluate the project.

Age range

- Birth to two year olds
- Three to four year olds

Artform

- Music

Background

First Notes is part of *sound52*, the project of Lincolnshire Youth Music Action Zone, one of 20 action zones set up by the National Foundation for Youth Music. The Youth Music Action Zone initiative provides a wide range of music-making opportunities for children and young people living in areas of social and economic need. One of the main tasks of *sound52* is to work in partnership with children, young people, their families and communities to build on existing strengths and help to give the children and young people greater confidence through music-making. It is estimated that more than half of those participating in *sound52* will not have had previous experience of music making.

Funding

The Music Action Zones receive Government funding. The Action Zone is also funded by Lincolnshire EYDCP, Lincolnshire Youth Music Service, East Midlands Arts, soundLINCS, the seven district councils in Lincolnshire, box office sales for the event. It is underwritten by Lincolnshire County Council.

The arts in the early years

Collaboration

sound52 is led by Lincolnshire County Council and soundLINCS in partnership with Lincolnshire Youth Service, Lincolnshire EYCDP, Lincolnshire Pre-school Learning Alliance, Arts Centres in Lincolnshire, YMCA and LAB Logic Records. It is supported by East Midlands Arts and all seven local authorities in Lincolnshire.

Reflections on the project by the organisers

Intended benefits and opportunities for young children

- Provides young children with the opportunity to experience music in a practical manner that may not be available to them otherwise
- Enables children to express themselves non-verbally through music and to become creative in an individual way
- Offers children a means of feeling encouraged, stimulated and open to new learning
- Fosters in children a sense of being included in the pre-school setting
- Increases the children's feeling of closeness with parents who have taken time to attend music-making activities in the pre-school setting

Intended benefits and opportunities for early years practitioners

- Offers the experience of working alongside professional artists
- Provides them with new skills they can apply to their work with young children
- Increases their sense of competence in creative activities
- Enables them to involve parents in activities thereby increasing the parent-practitioner partnership

Intended benefits and opportunities for artists

- Increases employment opportunities for musicians
- Provides musicians with experience of working in educational settings
- Offers the opportunity to gain skills in working with young children

Benefits to parents

- Demystifies the perception of music-making as 'not for them' or 'too expensive'
- Encourages participation in pre-school settings' activities
- Offers training in skills for music-making at home

Support for similar initiatives in the future

- Allow for longer timescales for the initial stages of putting arts projects into practice. It can take time to build up a group of people from the relevant sectors who have the necessary skills and knowledge to develop the project

sound52 is forward looking. It aims at building up a clientele for a future project which would involve the creation of a music-making centre and a travelling van with recording facilities. Funding for the centre would be sought from a variety of sources, including the European Union and the Arts Lottery.

Case study seven

Region:	West Midlands Arts
The project:	Artist in Residence
Organisers:	Hillfields Early Years Centre, Coventry

What is the project about?

- Taking forward ideas developed in the pre-schools of Reggio Emilia in Italy
- Encouraging creativity in the Centre
- Developing creative skills and raising self-esteem in children, parents and staff
- Taking part in planning, documenting, training and evaluation throughout the residency
- Disseminating the work in progress to early years practitioners in Coventry and Warwickshire
- The project culminates in an exhibition in the Herbert Gallery, Coventry

The current artist in residence started full time in January 2002 for a period of two school terms. The artist consulted the staff over the kinds of projects and themes they usually worked on and incorporated these in the art projects. For example, the current theme for the children aged three and four involves growth and living things. The artist explains the aims of the 'living things' art project as engaging children in the exploration of nature and how things grow; fostering curiosity and understanding of the natural world; and using a wide range of creative processes as a vehicle for expression.

Pictures and models of insects and small animals, for example frogs, butterflies, spiders etc. are recreated by the children using a variety of materials. Lasting for five weeks, the work is expected to culminate in a transparent wall hanging.

Age range and setting

- Birth to two year olds
- Two to three year olds
- Three to four year olds

The children attend Hillfields Early Years Centre, an Early Excellence Centre established in 1997 to meet the needs of a community in an inner-city area of Coventry. The population is a mixture of white English and Asian families, as well as a number of refugee families. The Centre is used by over 200 children and their families each week. For many children, English is a second language, while a number have special needs (especially behavioural problems or autism). These children in particular are regarded as benefiting from having an opportunity to express their feelings non-verbally through art.

Artform

- Visual Arts

Background

The Head of the Centre was inspired by the work in Reggio Emilia and by the underlying philosophy. The Centre's previous experience of working with a visual artist was so successful, albeit brief, that they were encouraged to appoint the current resident artist.

Funding

The artist in residence is funded through the Standards Fund for maintained nursery schools.

Collaboration

The Centre's staff work in collaboration with Coventry LEA, Warwickshire Arts and Education, Warwickshire EYDCP and the DfES.

Reflections on the project by the organisers and other participants

Benefits and opportunities for young children

- Offers young children the opportunity to work with a wider range of materials then before, for example using screen printing
- Develops their creative skills through focussed one-to-one or one-to-two input from the artist
- Increases their confidence and self-esteem and so makes them more independent
- Develops young children's motor control and observational skills
- Provides children with new ways of increasing their vocabulary and verbal abilities
- Offers the opportunity to express their feelings in non-verbal ways

Benefits and opportunities for early years practitioners

- Helps develop personal art skills through learning to work with new materials
- Provides new ideas and motivation through seeing how the children respond to the artist
- Offers a different perspective on working with young children

Benefits and opportunities for the artist

- Offers the opportunity to see the world from the children's perspective
- Knowledge of children's abilities and development
- Children have taught the artist new techniques she now uses in her own art work

- Recognition that for young children, the experience is often more important than the end product

    This is my ideal job

    Artist in residence

Benefits to parents

- Provides opportunities to consider children's high level of ability and competence
- Gives the opportunity to discuss with parents the long-term benefits of supporting children's creativity
- Increases their interest in the Centre's work and their children's development
- For the parents who attended the toddler group with their children, enjoyment of working with art materials themselves

Support for similar initiatives in the future

- Provide opportunities for more staff training so that the artist's work can be actively continued after the project has ended
- Artists should be engaged in a much wider range of pre-school settings

The Centre includes a parent-toddler group, a group for children under three and another group for children aged three and four. All three groups have enjoyed working with the resident artist, covering a variety of topics and using a wide range of materials and techniques. The entire Centre, including the parents, was in a state of excitement about an impending exhibition at Coventry's main art gallery in the Summer 2002. As well as the children's artwork, the exhibition showed a quilt made by the parent-toddler group. A second exhibition is scheduled for the summer of 2003 in London's International Gallery of Children's Art.

Case study eight

Region:	North West Arts
The project:	Early Years Creative Arts
Organisers:	Artists in Schools (AiS)

What is the project about?

- Providing children with positive and enjoyable experiences
- Offering children opportunities and the freedom to think, feel, communicate, explore, represent, express and reflect
- Developing children's creative, practical, personal and social skills
- Promoting greater awareness in parents and the local community of the role of creativity in children's learning and development
- Encouraging parents to regard themselves as valued partners in their children's education

- Helping parents to develop ideas for child-centred creative activities they can enjoy with their children
- Promoting in early years practitioners a greater understanding of the aesthetic and creative abilities of young children
- Encouraging practitioners to have increased confidence in planning and delivering creative activities as stepping stones towards the Early Learning Goals

Age range and setting

- Three and four year olds

The *Early Years Creative Arts* project is in its third year and will be completed by March 2003. The project involves 12 early years settings in an inner-city area of Bolton. Each setting hosts five artists' residencies. In addition, 'Creativity at Home' packs are being devised and will be distributed to parents in the area. Each artist's residency comprises a 'familiarisation visit' by the artist to the setting; a planning meeting; between six and ten sessions with the children; and an evaluation meeting.

Artforms

- Dance
- Music
- Mark making
- Textiles
- 3D artforms

Background and inspiration

Since 1998, AiS has promoted the involvement of visual artists, musicians, dancers, writers and drama practitioners in teaching and learning. A developing strand of AiS involves children at the Foundation Stage. The *Early Years Creative Arts* project in Bolton is one of four major early years projects in which AiS is currently involved. The others are in Bury, Rochdale and Tameside. The main aim of the Bolton Creative Arts project is to improve the quality of experiences of children living in an inner-city area. The project is managed by the Early Years Advisory service.

Funding

AiS is funded by the Local Authorities of Bolton, Bury and Rochdale. The Early Years Creative Arts project is funded by Sure Start.

Partnerships and collaboration

AiS works in partnership with the Early Years Advisory Service and EYDCP. The project relates closely to the Early Learning Goals for the Foundation Stage and promotes collaboration between the early years practitioners and the artists in order to fully utilise the expertise of both parties.

The arts in the early years

Reflections on the project by the organisers and other participants

Benefits and opportunities for young children

- Increases their confidence in their abilities and competence
- Develops their sense of creativity and imagination
- Develops their co-ordination and motor skills
- Encourages them to make choices and make their own decisions
- Teaches them to work as a team

> Building on children's interests and abilities is much more satisfying than drilling children for ballet exams.
>
> Resident dance artist and former ballet teacher

Benefits and opportunities for early years practitioners

- Offers them the opportunity to learn new skills and techniques from the artists
- Makes them aware of their own creative abilities
- Gives them a better understanding of the importance of developing children's creativity

> You learn a lot more from working alongside the artist and the children than from going on a course.
>
> Early years practitioner

Benefits and opportunities for artists

- Emphasises the importance of improvisation and adaptation
- Stresses the value of creativity for learning

Benefits to parents

- Increases their interest in the school and in what the children do there
- Helps them realise that learning is not only a matter of getting down to academic subjects
- Provides them with ideas of what to do at home and during holidays

Support for similar initiatives in the future

- Provide more funding for arts projects
- Convince primary school staff of the importance of building on early years creativity
- Emphasise the benefit of longer-term arts projects for children's creative development and for showing early years practitioners the value of creative experiences in the learning process

The arts in the early years

> Children need a balanced curriculum in which arts play a bigger role
>
> Early years Advisory Teacher

The project has created a positive working relationship between artists and pre-school practitioners. Both artists and practitioners were of the view that introducing arts projects into the curriculum has been very beneficial to the children and has increased the parents' involvement in the pre-school settings.

Case study nine

Region:	Southern and South East Arts
The project:	Early Years Story Tent
Organisers:	Silver Wheels Arts Company

What is the project about?

- Providing an easily accessible storytelling space for use with young children
- Creating a visually appealing space for storytelling with young children
- Involving young children in the production of interchangeable panels for the storytelling tent
- Encouraging young children to have a sense of ownership
- Offering a bookable, adaptable resource

The panel-making project took place in four early years settings on the Isle of Wight during March and April 2002. It involved the creation of appliqué panels depicting fairy stories (The Three Little Pigs, Jack and the Beanstalk, Cinderella) and nursery rhymes (Little Miss Muffet, Hey Diddle Diddle). The artist told the story, then discussed with the children what the panel should depict. Velcro was attached to the finished panels so that they could easily be removed and replaced by others. The panels decorated the outside of the tent, while the inside was made more interesting, homely and exciting through a canopy, floor cushions and the use of coloured lights. The tent with panels can be hired by early years settings and other organisations on the island.

Age range

- Birth to two year olds
- Three to four year olds

Artforms

- Visual arts and crafts including sewing, weaving, fabric printing

Background and inspiration

The idea for the storytelling tent arose initially from the Isle of Wight Council's arts officer in consultation with Sure Start Ryde and the Quay Arts Centre in Newport. A discussion with commissioned artists led to a series of workshops and the involvement of the Early Years department.

The arts in the early years

The commissioned artists, Silver Wheel Arts Company, is an island-based company with experience in delivering arts projects to family learning groups and schools. The artists are trained in teaching basic skills in mathematics and English to adults. They are also experienced in working with mixed age groups. Previous projects involved a variety of media including ceramics, mosaic, performing arts, feltmaking, silk painting and the production of carnival costumes and puppets.

Funding

The project was jointly funded by the IOW Council, The Quay Arts 'Moving On' fund, Sure Start Ryde and the Early Years Department.

Collaboration

The project was the result of collaboration between the artists, the early years co-ordinator at the Isle of Wight Council, Quay Arts Centre, Ryde Sure Start and EYDCP.

Reflections on the project by the organisers and other participants

Benefits and opportunities for young children

- Offers the opportunity to be involved in creative processes
- Allows learning from the process without worrying about the end product
- Encourages working in a group and learning from the group
- Gives young children confidence in their own abilities
- Provides young children with new experiences
- Increases language skills through storytelling

Benefits and opportunities for early years practitioners

- Gives practitioners confidence in their own creative abilities
- Encourages practitioners to work with the children on creative activities
- Provides new ideas and fresh perspectives for work with young children
- Encourages resourcefulness and flexibility
- Opens up new opportunities for working with and learning from others

Benefits and opportunities for artists

- Gives artists experience of gauging children's development and abilities
- Encourages artists to be flexible when working in different settings

Benefits to parents

- Encourages parental involvement in the early years setting
- Gives parents a chance to be creative themselves

Support for similar initiatives in the future

The arts in the early years

- Provide more designated support for creative activities
- Emphasise that children's learning from the process is more important than the end product
- Offer good evaluation programmes
- Convince early years practitioners of the value of early art projects

The *Story Tent* project is a good example of how two arts activities (panel making and storytelling) can be combined and how one arts activity (making tent panels) can then serve as a basis for another arts activity (story telling). The project also has the unique advantage of providing ongoing income, as the tent can be hired out to early years settings and other organisations.

Case study ten

Region:	East England Arts
The project:	ArtsStart
Organisers:	Essex County Council Cultural Services, Essex County Council Early Years, The Mercury Theatre and FirstSite Gallery, supported by East England Arts

What is the project about?

- Providing opportunities for the development of imagination, creative thinking and self-esteem for young children, particularly boys
- Enabling young children to work directly with professional artists using a range of artforms
- Develop the skills and level of understanding of the early years education sector about working with artists
- Develop the skills and level of understanding of artists about the early years sector
- Create a regional resource enabling the dissemination of good practice, including artists, resources, exemplars and pathways for implementation

ArtsStart is an early years training project for artists of differing disciplines and early years practitioners. A one-year pilot phase was completed in June 2002. Following national advertising, 12 artists were selected to work in mixed-gender, mixed-artform pairs in six early years settings. The artists and the early years practitioners received training: the artists about working with young children and the early years practitioners about the potential and value of artists in education. The training sessions were followed by five-week residencies for the artists. During this period each pair of artists delivered workshops in the early years settings, alongside the early years practitioners. Following an internal and external evaluation of this pilot stage, there are plans to develop and extend *ArtsStart* to include a wider geographical area and additional groups, including childminders, travellers and refugees. Funding is needed for this to continue.

Age range and settings

- Three to six year olds

The arts in the early years

This pilot stage of the project took place in six nursery schools or nursery classes in primary schools. Several of the schools were in areas of disadvantage and were facing pressures following OFSTED inspections.

Artforms

- Dance
- Drama
- Music
- Visual arts
- Literature
- Media/multi-media

Background and Inspiration

The project was conceived by Ronessa Knock from the Arts Education Service, Essex County Council.

> There was evidence of a clear need in Essex for artists with the skills and confidence to work with very young children. There were increasing requests from early years settings. We have many excellent artists working in education, but the majority were quite fearful of early years work without training.

Partnerships and collaboration

Following the initial idea for the project, partners joined across the arts and early years sectors. The LEA Early Years Support team was keen to encourage early years practitioners to work with artists and also to re-examine its own practice. East England Arts held an early years conference. Two arts organisations have also played important roles in the project: The Mercury Theatre and Firstsite at the Minories Art Gallery, Colchester. The project was managed by a part-time co-ordinator based at the Mercury Theatre.

Funding

Funding was received from Essex County Council (Early Years and Cultural Services), East England Arts, Community Safety Fund and Colchester Borough Council.

Reflections on the project by the organisers and other participants

What have been the benefits and opportunities for young children?

- Generated a sense of awe and wonder
- Enabled to explore and devise own ideas with more freedom than usual
- Increased their concentration span and focus by being totally engaged in activities

The arts in the early years

- Opportunities to work collaboratively with their peers and listen more to each other
- Created the means to communicate their feelings and demonstrated a growth in self-esteem and pride in their work
- Positive impact on the whole learning environment

> There were opportunities for the children to express themselves emotionally in varied ways. The artists themselves provided emotional havens.
>
> Early years practitioner

> They did learn something – they learned how to use their imagination
>
> Year 5 pupil about the nursery project

What have been the benefits and opportunities for early years practitioners?

- An understanding of the power of the arts as a learning tool
- Ability to be more flexible and open-minded and 'to take risks'
- Ability to be more child-centred
- Ability to expect the unexpected and to have higher expectations of young children
- The mutual benefits of working with artists:

> I have gained increasing confidence in my commitment that children (all of us really) have more to give than we know. The artists who worked with us were skilled developers who were also constantly delighted by the returns that were offered to them.
>
> Early years practitioner

What have been the benefits and opportunities for artists?

- Opportunities to talk to and work with other artists
- Increased understanding of young children
- Challenge to own practice in how ideas could be communicated

Support for similar initiatives in the future

- Provide funding so this model can be extended to other settings
- Encourage partnerships between Early Years and Cultural Services at a county level and partnerships with arts organisations
- Creative arts to be given more priority in school development plans

This pilot project presents an innovative model of training and residencies for artists and early years practitioners. It brings together expertise from local arts organisations, artists and the early years organisations. *ArtsStart* also demonstrates the importance of key individuals with knowledge and commitment to the arts and early years.